The Garland Library
of Medieval Literature

General Editors
James J. Wilhelm, Rutgers University
Lowry Nelson, Jr., Yale University

Literary Advisors
Ingeborg Glier, Yale University
Guy Mermier, University of Michigan
Fred C. Robinson, Yale University
Aldo Scaglione, University of North Carolina

Art Advisor
Elizabeth Parker McLachlan, Rutgers University

Music Advisor
Hendrik van der Werf, Eastman School of Music

Color illumination:
Christine de Pizan at her desk. Reproduced with permission of the Bibliothèque Nationale, Fonds Français 835, folio 1 recto.

Christine de Pizan

The Epistle of the Prison of Human Life

With An Epistle to the Queen of France *and* Lament on the Evils of the Civil War

edited and translated by
JOSETTE A. WISMAN

Volume 21
Series A
GARLAND LIBRARY OF MEDIEVAL LITERATURE

Garland Publishing, Inc.
New York & London
1984

Library of Congress Cataloging in Publication Data

Christine, de Pisan, ca. 1364–ca. 1431.
The epistle of the prison of human life ; with, An
epistle to the Queen of France ; and, Lament on the evils
of the civil war.

(Garland library of medieval literature ; v. 21.
Series A)
Bibliography: p.
Includes index.
1. Christine, de Pisan, ca. 1364–ca. 1431—
Translations, English. I. Wisman, Josette A. II. Title.
III. Series: Garland library of medieval literature ;
v. 21.
PQ1575.A28   1984   846'.2   83-49393
ISBN 0-8240-9412-3

Printed on acid-free, 250-year-life paper
Manufactured in the United States of America

The Garland Library
of Medieval Literature

To
Denise in memoriam and to Jon,
Pierre, Joseph, and Hazel

Preface of the General Editors

The Garland Library of Medieval Literature was established to make available to the general reader modern translations of texts in editions that conform to the highest academic standards. All of the translations are original, and were created especially for this series. The translations attempt to render the foreign works in a natural idiom that remains faithful to the originals.

The Library is divided into two sections: Series A, texts and translations; and Series B, translations alone. Those volumes containing texts have been prepared after consultation of the major previous editions and manuscripts. The aim in the editing has been to offer a reliable text with a minimum of editorial intervention. Significant variants accompany the original, and important problems are discussed in the Textual Notes. Volumes without texts contain translations based on the most scholarly texts available, which have been updated in terms of recent scholarship.

Most volumes contain Introductions with the following features: (1) a biography of the author or a discussion of the problem of authorship, with any pertinent historical or legendary information; (2) an objective discussion of the literary style of the original, emphasizing any individual features; (3) a consideration of sources for the work and its influence; and (4) a statement of the editorial policy for each edition and translation. There is also a Select Bibliography, which emphasizes recent criticism on the works. Critical writings are often accompanied by brief descriptions of their importance. Selective glossaries, indices, and footnotes are included where appropriate.

The Library covers a broad range of linguistic areas, including all of the major European languages. All of the important literary forms and genres are considered, sometimes in anthologies or selections.

The General Editors hope that these volumes will bring the general reader a closer awareness of a richly diversified area that has for too long been closed to everyone except those with precise academic training, an area that is well worth study and reflection.

James J. Wilhelm
Rutgers University

Lowry Nelson, Jr.
Yale University

Contents

Christine de Pizan at her desk, with three allegorical figures: Dame Reason, Dame Ryght-wytnesse, and Dame Justice, left to right, as identified in the *Cyte of Ladyes* (printed by Pepwell, 1521, signature Aai verso. (Courtesy of Folger Shakespeare Library)

Introduction

Life of the Author

Although many medieval writers say nothing about themselves in their works, let alone make mention of their names, we are fortunate that we are able to know most of Christine de Pizan's life through her works. She is not a mere carrier of a social rank, but a distinct personality, whose pride of authorship shines through all her writings.

In *L'Avision-Christine* (1405), Christine de Pizan tells her readers that she was born in Venice, where her father, known as Tommasso di Benvenuto da Pizzano, had gone to marry the daughter of a friend, who was a councilor of the city. The family name—Pizzano—derives from a little town near Bologna, the famous university city where Tommasso was educated and where he taught (Nicolini, p.145; references are keyed to the Select Bibliography). The friend was Tommasso di Mondino da Forlì, who had been a colleague of Christine's father at the university. Christine de Pizan was probably born in 1364, since she says in *L'Avision* that, at her husband's death in 1389, she was twenty-five. She had two younger brothers, Paolo and Aghinolfo. Several months after her birth, her father, who was then also a municipal councilor in Venice, moved his family back to Bologna. His gifts as a physician-astrologer attracted offers from the kings of France and Hungary, and he eventually accepted a post as official astrologer to Charles V. He left for France in 1364 and in 1368, Christine and the rest of the family joined him in Paris.

Shortly before her fifteenth birthday, Christine was married to Etienne de Castel, who later became a royal secretary. Tommasso, now known as Thomas de Pizan, or sometimes also as Thomas de Boulaigne, lost favor at court after the death of his benefactor in 1380. He died a few years later, probably between 1385 and 1389. It is also in 1389, in October or November, that Etienne de Castel succumbed to an epidemic in Beauvais. Christine had borne him three children, a girl in 1381, and two boys, one of whom must have died in infancy, while the other one, Jehan, was born around 1385.

At the age of twenty-five, Christine de Pizan was thus a widow, providing for herself, her children, her mother, and her two brothers until the latter returned to Italy in 1394. Although both her father and husband had apparently left her a small inheritance, she informs us in *L'Avision* that the legacies included debts as well, which kept her entangled in several lawsuits for a number of years. As a remedy for all these misfortunes, this extraordinary woman turned to writing, both to gain her livelihood and to satisfy her love of study.

Christine tells her readers that she had been well taught by her father in spite of her sex, and that she became determined to put her knowledge and talents to good use. Although she explicitly dates the beginning of her writing to 1399, we know from her own hand that she composed ballades, virelais, and rondeaux before that date. She tells us in *L'Avision*, that in 1398 the Earl of Salisbury, having heard of her poetry and appreciating it greatly, took Christine's son—then thirteen years of age—to England to be educated with his own son. Nevertheless, it may be significant that the poetess neglects to mention her first literary attempts in her later works. She may have thought that she wrote these early poems of love and the joy of loving to cover her sadness and regret after the death of a much-loved husband. From 1399 to 1429, she wrote more courtly poetry, epistles, and long didactic treatises in prose and verse.

Christine de Pizan lived in troubled times. The Hundred Years War was still raging, and the English invaded France in 1415; a civil war broke out between the Houses of Orléans and Burgundy while Charles VI went mad; there were peasant and bourgeois revolts; the Church was divided by the Great Schism; and finally there were recurring epidemics and famines. In the midst of this chaos, Christine committed herself to struggle against the vices of the time. Excluded from the university and political affairs by her sex, she nevertheless showed herself to be a well-read woman who wanted to involve herself in the political affairs of the time. The themes of the role of women in society, the necessity of a good education for them, of peace and conciliation between the classes and royal houses in the French Kingdom appear very early in her works and become the subsequent leitmotifs of her long treatises and epistles.

In 1399 and 1400, she wrote some short poems, *Quinze Joies de Nostre-Dame*, *Le Debat des deux amans*, *Le Livre des trois jugements amoureux*, two *Oraisons*, *Les Dits moraux*, and *Les Enseignements de Christine a son fils Jehan*. In 1399 Christine also wrote the *Epistre au dieu d'Amours*, an attack against Ovid and especially Jean de Meung's *Roman de la Rose*, an epistle which started a quarrel in which the humanists of the day, Jean de Montreuil, Gontier and Pierre Col, Guillaume de Tignonville, and the chancellor of the University of Paris, Jean Gerson, took part. With this work, Christine began her lifelong defense of women against slander. This quarrel was continued in the *Dit de la Rose*, written in 1402. The letters of the quarrel were then presented to the Queen of France, Isabella.

Women were also the heroines of Christine de Pizan's first long didactic work, *L'Epistre d'Othea a Hector* (circa 1400–1401), in which only thirty-three stories out of one hundred do not give principal importance to women (see Campbell, *L'Epître*). *Le Livre de la mutacion de Fortune*—written between August 1400 and November 1403—is 23,336 lines long, with a lengthy chapter in prose; it narrates the blows of Fortune in history and contains a mine of information on Christine, her parents, and her husband. Before finishing the *Mutacion de Fortune*, it took her less than one year (October 1402 to March 1403) to compose *Le Chemin de lonc estude*, another long work in verse which is a dream vision modeled in parts after Dante's *Divine Comedy*. In it, Christine, guided by the Cumean Sybil, goes from this world to a better one, where she will discover the "fountain of wisdom," and try to correct the evils created by men. In 1403 also, Christine wrote *Le Dit de la pastoure*, another sad love story, this time between a prince and a lowly *pastoure* (shepherdess).

In 1404, Christine, asked by Philip the Bold of Burgundy to write a biography of his father, composed *Le Livre des fais et bonnes meurs du sage roy Charles V*, a long laudatory work of her father's benefactor. The year 1405 witnessed the completion of several more of her most important works. Among these is *Le Livre de la cité des dames*, which is justly considered one of her most "feminist" pieces and the first work by a woman in praise of women. In the City of Ladies that three allegorical figures named Reason, Rectitude, and Justice commission Christine to build are found all the honorable women from the past and present who have been very often unfairly forgotten or slandered in stories composed by men. A follow-up to the *Cité des dames* is the *Livre des trois vertus*, an instructional work of behavior for women of all classes.

L'Avision-Christine, also dated from 1405, is, with *La Mutacion de Fortune*, one of the principal sources of biographical data on Christine. In the third book of *L'Avision*, Christine narrates to Dame Philosophy the story of her life, and accepts the comfort given to her by the lady. This work can be seen also as the first of Christine's appeals for peace, since in it she deplores the evils of war. In a second work, composed on October 1405, the *Epistre a la royne*, Christine implores Queen Isabella to settle the differences between the dukes of Orléans and Burgundy, to understand the sufferings of the French people, and to avert an English victory in France. In 1405, Christine de Pizan also wrote a long romance in verse, *Le Livre du duc des vrais amans*. It relates the story of a young duke in love with his married cousin. The heroes have sometimes been recognized as John of Bourbon and Mary of Berry, to whom the *Epistre de la prison de vie humaine* was later addressed. In the romance, the two lovers part; in real life, John was to become Mary's third husband. This was Christine's last work in the courtly-love tradition.

It is probably between 1405 and 1406 that *Le Livre de prudence* and its second version renamed *Le Livre de la prod'hommie de l'homme* were written. These works are a paraphrased translation of the *De quattuor virtutibus* of the Pseudo-Seneca. More original is the *Livre du corps de policie* completed in 1407; it is a political and instructional work, a mirror for princes, and the prince, in this case, is the dauphin Louis of Guyenne. In it, several passages deal with the misfortunes of perennial war. A treatise on the art of warfare, *Le Livre des fais d'armes et de chevalerie* followed the *Corps de policie*; its most important source was Vegetius' *De re militari*, the only complete Roman treatise known on the Roman army. In the same year, 1410, Christine wrote *Les sept psaumes allegorisés* that she presented to the Duke of Berry in January. In August, she again exhorted the Duke in her *Lamentacion sur les maux de la guerre civile* to work for peace. In the

Lamentacion, Christine deplores once again the evils of the war that had broken out between the followers of the Armagnacs and Burgundians after the so-called peace of Chartres (signed in 1409). Her eloquence must have been heard, for on November 2, 1410, the peace of Bicêtre was signed.

Christine mentioned in her *Livre de la paix* (1414), that she had written an *Avision du coq* the preceding year, but this work has been lost. *Le Livre de la paix,* offered again to the dauphin, is another guidebook for the edification of the young prince. It is not without resemblance to the *Livre du corps de policie,* written seven years before. Christine is then silent for four years, although she said in the *Epistre de la prison de vie humaine* (1418) that she had begun its composition much earlier, but that "worries and troubles of the heart" had prevented her from completing it more rapidly. This consolatory epistle was addressed to Mary of Berry and to all women of the French kingdom who had lost their kinsmen through battle (particularly Agincourt) or by natural death.

In 1418, Jehan de Castel, Christine's son, married Jeanne Le Page (see Pinet, p.174). Unfortunately, this happy event occurred in a year marked by tragic events: John the Fearless, who had recognized since October 1416 Henry V of England as the legal heir of the French throne, stood by while Henry starved the besieged population of Rouen, and subsequently conquered the whole of Normandy. In Paris, more than five hundred Armagnacs were murdered on the night of May 28. Bernard d'Armagnac was killed on June 12 along with 1600 of his followers. Another massacre occurred on August 20, and an epidemic killed tens of thousands shortly after this last massacre. The party of the Armagnacs was thus completely annihilated, and the dauphin, the future Charles VII, left the capital to seek refuge in Melun. His followers were arrested, and many executed. In view of these tragic events and Christine's loyalty to the dauphin, it is not surprising that Christine should flee the capital to find refuge in a convent. There she wrote her last known work, *Le Ditié de la pucelle,* dated July 31, 1429. In it, Christine said that she had been in this "abbey" for the past eleven years. The *Ditié* is one of the very few homages rendered to Joan of Arc while she was still alive. The tone of the poem is one of joy and satisfaction in a peace brought about by the appearance on the political scene of this miraculous young woman from Lorraine.

In between the *Epistre de la prison de vie humaine* and the *Ditié*, we still have another work by Christine de Pizan entitled *Les Heures de contemplacion sur la passion de Nostre-Seigneur*. The exact date of this work is not known; however, Suzanne Solente (in "Un traité inédit") suggested that—given the subject matter of the *Heures*, its sad tone, and the fact that Christine spoke to the ladies afflicted by the misfortunes of the time as she said she had already done in the past—the *Heures de contemplacion* was written after the *Epistre de la prison*, probably around 1420. It has been assumed that Christine de Pizan died shortly after writing the *Ditié de la pucelle*, and before the death of Joan of Arc in 1431. It seems reasonable to suppose that, had she outlived Joan of Arc's death in good health, she would have written about her.

Christine de Pizan was well known and read by many in her own time. The number of manuscripts of her works that have come down to us is impressive: we have more than forty manuscripts of *L'Epistre d'Othea*, twenty-five of *Le Livre de la cité des dames*, seventeen of *Le Livre des trois vertus*, to mention only a few of her works. She had a wide range of patrons, among them: Charles VI and Queen Isabella, Philip and John of Burgundy, Louis of Orléans, and above all John of Berry, whose library included most of her works (see M. Meiss, P. Delisle). But as Charity C. Willard has pointed out in *The Manuscript Tradition*, her audience was not exclusively aristocratic: a large number of her manuscripts, which were written on coarse paper and were crudely illustrated, were intended for the bourgeoisie. It is also worth noting that, whether intended for aristocratic or bourgeois audiences, a number of her works (especially *Le Livre des trois vertus*) took up concerns of women of all classes.

We have seen that, in her adopted country, Christine enjoyed the patronage of the mightiest, and in her engagement in the literary battle over *Le Roman de la Rose*, she was recognized even by her opponents as a wise and highly intelligent woman. Another of her contemporary fellow writers, Eustache Deschamps, wrote a ballad in her honor (ca. 1404); in the first stanza, Deschamps wrote (French original in Towner, *L'Avision*, p.13):

> Eloquent muse in between the nine, Christine,
> You have no equal that I know today;
> You have acquired wisdom in all your learning;

You received your knowledge from none other but God;
Your epistles and books, which I have read
In many places, are full of high philosophy,
And what you wrote to me one time
Makes me believe in the great abundance
Of your knowledge, which increases forever;
You are unique in your accomplishments in the kingdom of
France.

In 1442, Martin Le Franc in his *Champion des dames* compared her to Cicero and Cato (French original in Pinet, p.454):

She was Tully and Cato:
Tully, since in eloquence
She had the rose and the bud;
Cato, because of her wisdom.

Jean Mielot was inspired by the *Epistre d'Othea* to write his *Cent Histoires de Troie* in 1461, and it is under this last title that the *Epistle* was printed successively in about 1499 by Philippe Pigouchet, in 1518 by the widow of Jean Trepperel, and in 1522 by Philippe Le Noir. In these editions, "Chrestienne" is the name given to the author, and in 1527, when Philippe Le Noir printed *L'Art de chevalerie selon Vegece*, following an earlier edition by Antoine Verard (1488), the author's name was not even mentioned. *Le Livre des trois vertus* was printed three times, under the title *Le Tresor de la cité des dames selon dame Christine*, first in 1497 by Antoine Verard, in 1503 by Michel Le Noir, and by Denis Janot and Jehan André in 1536. Finally in 1549, *Le Chemin de long estude de dame Cristine de Pise* was translated "from Romance into French" by Jean Chaperon and printed by Estienne Groulleau (see Thomassy, pp.93–94).

Suzanne Solente (in "Deux chapitres") noted that Christine's literary influence lasted well until the middle of the sixteenth century. Unfortunately, Christine de Pizan's works were practically ignored for centuries thereafter. However, in her own lifetime and many years after her death, Christine's fame went beyond the borders of France. She played an important role in the world of belles-lettres in England. The Earl of Salisbury first heard of Christine's poetry, and, as she said in *L'Avision*, appreciated it since he himself was a "gracious poet." Her son Jehan was sent to England to be educated with the Earl's son. After the decapitation of Salisbury, who had taken sides with Richard II, Jehan was given protection by the new king, Henry IV. He remained in England for three years. Christine's renown as a poet was then established at the English court as early as 1400.

A few English writers, namely Thomas Hoccleve, William Worcester, and the author of the *Assembly of Gods* (see Bühler, *The Assembly of Gods*), borrowed from Christine in their works. *L'Epistre d'Othea* and *Le Livre du corps de policie* were the first works of Christine to be translated in English. *The Epistle of Othea* was first translated by Stephen Scrope for his father-in-law Sir John Falstoff, in around 1440. A second translation was made in the first years of the sixteenth century by Anthony Babyngton. Around 1540, a third printed translation was done by Robert Wyer (see *The Epistle of Othea*, ed. Bühler, intro. 12–25, and ed. Gordon, intro. 21–25). *The Book of the Body of Polycie* was translated twice: the first translation dates from the middle of the fifteenth century; the second was done by Robert Wyer, who printed it in 1521. William Caxton printed translations of Christine's *Proverbes moraux* in 1478, and of *Le Livre des fais d'armes et de chevalerie* in 1489. In 1526, R. Pynson reprinted Caxton's edition of *The Morale Proverbes*. A translation of *Le Livre de la cité des dames* was printed in 1521 by Henry Pepwell. However, Christine de Pizan's works were equally popular in their French originals in England. P.G.C. Campbell in "Christine de Pisan en Angleterre" remarked that her popularity can be measured by the number of French manuscripts of various works extant in England. Campbell discovered twelve of them in the British Library and four at the Bodleian Library at Oxford. We should add to these the *Epistre a la royne*, which is contained in All Souls MS 182 at Oxford.

Christine's fame in England was well established and long-lasting. But she was also well known in other countries. Although we do not find any of her works in French or Italian in her native country, we know in her *Avision* that Gian Galeazzo Visconti, the duke of Milan, had invited her to his court. She refused because she was in the midst of legal problems, and as she said, she would not have left France with "a light heart," even to go to her "natural country" (see *L'Avision*, ed. Towner, p.166).

Her works in defense and praise of women were translated into other languages in the late fifteenth century. In Flanders, the *Livre*

de la cité des dames (Stede der vrouwen) was translated about
1475. In Portugal, *Le Livre des trois vertus (O Livre das tres ver-
tudes)* appeared in the middle of the fifteenth century. This translation was printed in 1518 under the title *Espelho de Christina.* To
our knowledge, there were no Spanish translations of Christine's
works, but M. Laigle (pp.40–41) noted that Luis Vivès in his *De
institutione christianae feminae* of 1523 and Christoval de Acosta
in his *Tratado en l'onor de las muyeres* (1592) borrowed heavily
from *Le Livre des trois vertus.*

In the second half of the nineteenth century, when a scientific
approach to medieval texts and authors emerged, the works of
Christine de Pizan came under close scrutiny. With the pioneering
studies of Marie-Josèphe Pinet, Mathilde Laigle, and especially
Suzanne Solente in this century, Christine de Pizan is no longer a
neglected author of the "Dark Ages." Many scholars in France,
Italy, and particularly in this country have recently worked toward
re-establishing her importance and an appreciation of the respect
and admiration that she once commanded. Most of her works are
now available in modern editions, and with this new edition of
three of her shorter pieces, there remain only three works—namely
Le Livre de prudence, Le Livre des fais d'armes et de chevalerie,
and *Les Heures de contemplacion sur la passion de Nostre-Seigneur*—which still lack a modern editor's attentive study.

Artistic Achievement

The three works of Christine de Pizan (often formerly spelled Pisan)
presented in this volume are epistles, and although the *Lamentacion sur les maux de la guerre civile* (Lamentation on the Evils of
the Civil War) does not bear the word itself in the title, it is nevertheless addressed to John of Berry. This genre was frequently used
by the author (see Pinet, who devotes a whole chapter to Christine
de Pizan's epistles, pp.263–80). *L'Epistre de la prison de vie humaine* (The Epistle of the Prison of Human Life) belongs to the
literary type called *consolatio*, which attempts to remedy the maladies of the soul. The origin of this type is Greek and philosophical
in its approach, but, as we shall see later, Christine's epistle is more
theological than philosophical. Her sources are to be found more

often in the Holy Scriptures and the Church Fathers' writings than in ancient philosophers' works.

Christine addresses the *Epistle* to Mary of Berry, Duchess of Bourbon, daughter of the generous patron John of Berry. Christine wants to console the Duchess, who, like many other noble women, has suffered the loss of several members of her family: a son-in-law, Philip of Burgundy, Count of Nevers; three cousins, Anthony of Burgundy, the Duke of Brabant; the Constable of Albret; and John of Arcourt, Duke of Aumale, all killed on that black day of October 25, 1415, in the ill-conceived Battle of Agincourt. And to compound Mary's grief, her own husband, John of Bourbon, and one of her sons (by her second husband, Philip of Artois), Charles, Count of Eu, had been taken prisoners by the English during that battle.

However, Christine makes clear near the beginning of her epistle that she had not originally intended to dedicate her work to Mary of Berry. The work had been commissioned by someone else, but the text itself does not yield any clue about the identity of Christine's commissioner. Suzanne Solente (in "Un traité inédit," pp.270–71) argued that the work was probably commissioned by Mary's father, John of Berry, but since he had died in 1416, Christine offered it to the daughter instead. However, this hypothesis seems improbable: it is unlikely that, if indeed John of Berry had originally commissioned the work, Christine would not have given him mention. John of Berry had been an exceedingly generous patron, and Christine had previously dedicated several works to him, notably *Les sept psaumes allegorisés*, written in 1409, and the *Lamentacion sur les maux de la guerre civile* in 1410; in the *Epistre de la prison de vie humaine* Christine praises John of Berry as "the excellent Duke," and adds that, prior to his death, she had sent him "little writings and epistles of mine." Thus, if John of Berry had originally commissioned this work, this would have been an ideal point at which Christine might acknowledge it. As to why Christine finally dedicated her work to Mary (in preference to any other grieving noble woman), it is impossible to answer. But this was not the first work offered to Mary of Berry; previously, Christine had presented her with a ballad written between 1400 and 1410 (see Roy, *Oeuvres Poétiques*, 1, 229–30).

Since the Battle of Agincourt and the circumstances that led up to it have been extensively treated by Nicolas, Hibbert, and Seward, only a few observations need to be made here. The battle lasted but three hours, during which the French suffered enormous casualties. Christopher Hibbert estimated that there were between 7000 and 10,000 casualties on the French side. In addition, approximately 1500 to 1600 French prisoners were taken to England, among them, as noted earlier, the husband and one son of Mary of Berry. John of Bourbon was to die a prisoner in England in 1434. Mary's son was eventually released in 1438.

The Battle of Agincourt was recorded in several histories in the fifteenth century: the French chronicles of Enguerrand de Monstrelet, of Jean Le Fevre, of Jehan de Wavrin, of the "religieux" of St. Denys, and the *Histoire de Charles VI* by Jouvenal des Ursins; for the English chronicles, see Nicolas and Hibbert. A good number of English poems were written to celebrate King Henry V's victory and his triumphant return to England. The best known of these English poems was written by John Lydgate, and is commonly entitled *The Siege of Harfleur and the Battle of Agincourt* (see Nicolas, pp.66–77). In France, the literary pieces written on the occasion of this defeat have been much less numerous. Enguerrand de Monstrelet in his *Chronicle* gives the text of a short poem of three stanzas written by "certain clerks of the realm of France," in which Henry V is blamed for his cruelty in giving the order that all the French wounded be executed (in *Enguerrand*, 3, 123–24). Aside from Christine de Pizan's *Epistre de la prison de vie humaine*, the only major work concerning the Battle of Agincourt was Alain Chartier's 3531-line poem, *Le Livre des quatre dames*, written in 1416. Chartier's poem concerns the plight of four ladies, all wives of knights who were at the Battle of Agincourt: the first lady has lost a husband who died a brave knight; the husband of the second has been taken prisoner by the English; the third one does not know the fate that befell her husband; and the last lady is shamed by the cowardly attitude of her husband, who fled the fight. These fictitious ladies engage in a casuistic debate, as each claims to be the most worthy of pity. The poet then submits their accounts to his beloved lady, who shall judge the debate. Chartier's attacks on the behavior of many knights at the battle reveal a deep concern for the decay of chivalric virtues—a concern which we do not find in the epistle of Christine de Pizan written two years later (it was finished in January of 1418, by the new calendar).

The title *L'Epistre de la prison de vie humaine* is derived, as Christine de Pizan informs us, from a comparison drawn by St. Bernard in his sermon *De virtute oboedientia et septem ejus gradibus* (see Migne, *Patrologia Latina 183*, col. 659). This long epistle is divided into twelve chapters, followed by a conclusion. The introductory chapter is written to remind Mary of Berry and all women who have suffered the losses of kin about our mortal condition and to have patience in adversity. In the next chapter numerous examples of how cruel men are punished in this world are given. Since the men whose losses these women lament were not cruel, Christine will give them five reasons for not grieving and for bearing with patience the blows inflicted on human life, which must be regarded as a prison. In the third chapter, the first two reasons are given: these valorous men died with the grace of God, and have thus escaped this prison. The third reason—that, given death's inevitability, it should not be feared—is contained in the fourth chapter. Between the third and fourth reasons, Christine offers and extols the virtue of two remedies which can soften Mary's grief: the first is to have hope in God, and the second is to have patience.

The fourth reason which should comfort those who have lost their friends is to be found in three kinds of gifts that we all receive: the gifts of grace, the gifts of nature, and the gifts of fortune (Chapter 7). These gifts are featured frequently in discussions about the definition of the *summum bonum* (highest good), starting with Aristotle's explanation of the Platonic theory which Christine de Pizan mentions when she discusses the gifts of grace *(bona animi)*. The gifts of nature *(bona corporis)* and the gifts of fortune *(bona fortunae)* are dealt with by Christine without the help of quotations. She stresses the good use of the gifts of fortune, since it is with these practical gifts that powerful men and women can do good to others who have not received these gifts. She turns to Mary of Berry in the next chapter to remind her that she has been particularly well endowed with the gifts of fortune. She encourages her to set a public example by giving alms to the poor and going on pilgrimages. Although Mary may be distressed since her husband and son have been taken prisoners by the English, she should rejoice in the company of her remaining children, Bonne, Catherine, Charles, and Louis.

Christine had shown in the second chapter how harsh God's

judgment would be on cruel men. In the ninth, she now says that the men who died well will be saved on Judgment Day, and they will enter the City of Paradise. This is the fifth reason why we should not mourn for our dead, as Christine says in the tenth chapter. The following two chapters describe the Holy City of Paradise and the joys of the blessed, which she compares to a crown of twelve stars. The last star—the vision of God—calls forth a quotation of St. Bernard about this glorious moment. Christine ends her epistle with a short paragraph in which she expresses her hope for success concerning her attempt to demonstrate that life after death will be more rewarding than this one for those who deserve it. She also begs Mary not to think badly of her for her tardiness in finishing this epistle.

Christine de Pizan has studded her work with quotations, not so much as to follow a tradition as to try to persuade her readers. Nevertheless, her sincerity in empathizing with Mary's grief cannot be doubted, since Christine herself had had to suffer many personal losses. Her love for her patrons, her adopted country, and her hatred of the war can be seen throughout the text as they were seen in her shorter works a few years before.

The *Epistre a la royne* (Epistle to the Queen), written in 1405, is a short prose piece followed by an unfinished rondeau in one manuscript. In the rondeau, Christine de Pizan declares that she was in a hurry to finish this epistle, and an examination of the text suggests that it may indeed have been written very rapidly. Gone are the many quotations that she normally uses to sustain her point, and a tone of informality permeates the work—that of one woman confiding her deep feelings in another. This informality, however, was cautious enough not to violate the deference due to a queen. As Christine says at the onset, she is in search of a remedy, any good remedy, to put a stop to the civil war in France. Since the queen might not be fully aware of the ruin brought about by this disastrous war, Christine will try to make her cognizant of this fact by personally appealing to her. If the queen can stop the deadly feud between the men of Orléans and the Burgundians, she will attain three goods pertaining to the soul: she will stop the shedding of brotherly blood, she will bring peace to all, and she will be remembered for it in the chronicles of the time. Christine de Pizan reminds the queen of the brave feats of noble ladies in history who obtained

peace against all odds. She ends her epistle by appealing to the
queen's patriotic refusal to let the French kingdom be divided.

The *Lamentacion*, written five years later, is another emotional
cry for peace. Christine starts by using the *ubi sunt* topos, claiming
that the noble kingdom of France has lost the men and women who
had made this country glorious and exemplary. A series of exhorta-
tions follows: Christine asks the knights to remember the chivalric
ideals which now seem lost; she asks the clerics to come and offer
their good and wise advice to the royal council; she asks the queen
and all women to open their eyes and hearts to try to appease the
deadly anger of the ambitious men who are fighting each other;
finally, she appeals to John of Berry particularly to be the mediator
for a peace. Because the duke is now the oldest, and therefore the
wisest, man in the royal family, and does not have any hatred in his
heart, he should come to Paris and attempt to stop the impending
battle between the factions. A victory on any side, given the circumstances, says Christine, would not be honorable. Again, in the *Lamentacion*, Christine uses very few historical examples and quotations. She is direct and pressing, because it is important to use time
to avoid more bloodshed. The many interjections used in this epistle reinforce her distress and horror at the present situation, at
seeing her beloved adopted country fallen into ruin and shame.

Christine de Pizan's sensitivity toward the horrors of war, the
grief of the mourning women, and the miseries of the common
people is eloquently shown in these three original works. Struc-
turally, the *Epistre de la prison de vie humaine*, a work which the
author would edit and rewrite often during its long composition, is
well balanced and flows harmoniously, in spite of the numerous
quotations. The first author quoted is St. Bernard, who is also the
last one to be quoted. The division into twelve chapters is recalled
in the twelve stars of the crown of the blessed in the last chapter.
Both the *Epistre a la royne* and the *Lamentacion* are emotional
pieces which were written with passionate feelings.

The style used by Christine de Pizan in the *Epistre de la prison
de vie humaine* has sometimes been deemed obscure (see Pinet,
pp.446–47). It is true that her use of syntax is very close at times to
Latin usage, and this makes the text difficult to read not only for the
modern reader, but for her contemporaries as well. Müller (in *Zur
Syntax*, pp.55–58) made particular mention of her frequent use of
the subjunctive. However, it should be noted that this difficult style

was not peculiar to Christine de Pizan. When in the middle of the fourteenth century more and more scholars were called upon to translate the classics, a frenzy to imitate anything Latin (be it vocabulary or syntax) seems to have possessed the French writers, and Christine de Pizan was not immune to it. It is to be noted, though, that the same critic who complained about Christine de Pizan's obscure style nevertheless recognized that it was motivated by a desire to elevate the French language to the subtleties of its Latin model.

There is nothing obscure or inelegant in Christine de Pizan's two shorter epistles. Their prose seems to flow naturally, as opposed to the more complicated syntax of the *Epistre*. Her vocabulary does not borrow as heavily from Latin. We even find examples of what has been noted as peculiar to her (see Gay, "On the Language", p.7), her heavy use of diminutives: "seulette," "femmelette," and so on. To sum up the merits of these three original works, we might turn to Earl Jeffrey Richards' introduction to *The Book of the City of Ladies*, p.21, where he noted that Christine's "style reflects the experimental and innovative nature of her prose. . . . She was both a writer and a scholar, welding together an enormous creative drive and a deep love of learning. To say anything less of Christine is to do her a profound disservice."

Sources and Influences

In her 1924 article, Suzanne Solente gave a partial edition of the text: specifically the eighth and thirteenth chapters, none of the tenth, and a few selected lines from the remaining ten chapters. This very incomplete edition was preceded by a long and meticulous study of Christine de Pizan's life and works and the circumstances which led the author to write such an epistle. Perhaps the greatest value of Suzanne Solente's article is her thorough examination of the biblical sources of the text, which have been used in preparing this complete edition of Christine de Pizan's *Epistre de la prison de vie humaine*. It has been necessary at times to correct some of the sources given by Solente and some missing sources have been found. However, in a few instances, some quotations have remained impossible to identify.

In the *Epistre de la prison de vie humaine,* the author claims that her own comforting words might not suffice to console Mary of Berry. To convince her to be patient in her grief, she draws on various writings which might help the distraught duchess. She tells Mary that she must put her faith in the Holy Scripture and many glorious doctors and sages. Before examining these three categories, we should note that, as has been pointed out frequently by modern editors, Christine often used compilations and anthologies that were popular in her days in lieu of the original works. Her some-times derivative and incomplete quotations also suggest that she frequently drew upon memory.

The Holy Scriptures: Christine quotes or makes reference to the following passages in the Bible: Genesis 4.16–24; Judges 4.21–22, 8.21, 9.53; 1 Kings 1.21, 8.21, 16.18, 22.38; 2 Kings 11; 2 Chroni-cles 23.21, 24.20–22; Judith 13.6–9; 1 Samuel 31.4; 2 Samuel 4.12, 18.9–15; 2 Maccabees 9.28; Job 14.1–2, 27; Psalms 31.7; Ecclesiastes 7.2; Ecclesiasticus 4.33; Ezekiel 21.30; Matthew 5.10, 18.6–7, 26.52; Mark 9.41; Luke 6.27, 17.3, 35; John 10.14, 20.29; Romans 12.12; Hebrews 11.6,13.14; Revelation 14.13. We should note that the quotations and references are very seldom taken directly from the Vulgate.

The glorious doctors: Christine de Pizan quotes from the fol-lowing patristic works, sometimes from the originals, but often from translations: Augustine's *Confessions* and *City of God;* Gre-gory the Great's *Moralia in Job* and the *Homeliae in evangelia* (both translated anonymously); Bernard de Clairvaux' *De virtute oboedientia et septem ejus gradibus, De proemio patriae coelestis,* and from his sermons. She quotes from Isidore of Seville's *Syn-onyma,* Anselm's *Proslogium seu alloquium de Dei existentia,* from Basil's epistles, and from Priscian's popular *Institutiones gram-maticae* (anonymous translation).

As for sage authorities, in the *Epistre de la prison* the most frequently quoted author is the Pseudo-Seneca's *De remediis for-tuitorum.* It is not possible to determine definitively whether Chris-tine translated directly from the Latin original or used the transla-tion done by Jacques Bauchans, or even drew excerpts from compilations such as Vincent de Beauvais' *Speculum historiale.* We do know that when Christine discusses the virtue of prudence, she used the Pseudo-Seneca's *De quattuor virtutibus*. This is another example of the use of moral teachings by pagan authors to support Christian doctrine.

Christine often quotes from Boethius' *Consolation of Philosophy*. She used this work extensively in some of her previous works, not only through quotations, but by borrowing the allegorical figure of Philosophy. This is evident in her *Chemin de lonc estude* and especially in *L'Avision*. Again, it would be difficult to determine if she quoted from the original or from the many French translations of this work.

M.-J. Pinet (p.266) thought that Christine had also borrowed from Vincent de Beauvais' *Consolatio pro morte amici* or from the French translation made in 1374. The chapters that the critic believed were "copied" by Christine, namely 12 through 16, describe the joys of the blessed. Both Vincent de Beauvais' chapters and Chapter 12 of *L'Epistre de la prison de vie humaine* are a presentation of Christian eschatology. Neither writer was very original in dealing with this subject.

Christine mentions other "wise authors": Aristotle (frequently used in the *Dits des Philosophes* by Guillaume de Tignonville); Quintilian, probably from the popular *Institutio oratoria*; Plato, from the *Phaedo* (to be found also in Guillaume de Tignonville); Lactantius; Ovid; Prosper, from the *Epigrammatum liber*; Florus; Josephus; Macrobius, from the *Commentary on the Dream of Scipio*; Theodolus from the *Ecloga*; Secundus; Albertus Magnus' *De arte moriendi*; and Maximianus from the *Elegia*. These were all very particular authors in the late Middle Ages.

In many of her works Christine mentioned several compilations of sayings by ancient or Christian authors. In the *Epistre de la prison* also, she may have used Valerius Maximus' *Dicta et facta memorabilia* (translated by Simon de Hesdin and Nicolas de Gonesse), the *Gesta et dicta antiquorum philosophorum* by Johannes Procida (translated as *Les Dits des Philosophes* by Guillaume de Tignonville), and Vincent de Beauvais' *Speculum historiale*. In the *Epistre a la royne*, Christine's quotations are not numerous. She briefly relates the story of Veturia, Coriolanus' mother, from Livy, probably from the translation by Pierre de Bersuire (created for John the Good); she mentions Queen Olympias,

Alexander's mother; and Queen Esther and Queen Blanche of Castile, all of whom can be also found in *Le Livre de la cité des dames* and *La Mutacion de Fortune*.

In the *Lamentacion sur les maux de la guerre civile*, Christine recalls the story of Polynices' widow, Argia, whom she had placed in her *City of Ladies*. The stories of many of the ladies in that city were taken from Boccaccio's *De mulieribus claris*, a borrowing that Christine acknowledged in her work. All the other characters evoked by Christine are to be found in her previous writings. The allusion to the Guelphs and the Ghibellines reminds us of Christine's Italian background.

As noted above, two of the three epistles exist in only one manuscript, while the third exists in only four. It is therefore reasonable to presume that these texts have had few readers. To our knowledge, they have neither been used nor referenced by Christine's epigones. But this statement applies to most of Christine's works. Her influence has been very limited, and the fact that she was a woman may not be totally foreign to her short-lasting renown. However, these three epistles are all original works which were destined for a small audience, in this case, the court of France. Even if the *Epistre a la royne* and the *Lamentacion sur les maux de la guerre civile* can be called spontaneous works, and the *Epistre de la prison de vie humaine* a more elegant and elaborate piece, they are all personal documents from a woman who gave spiritual advice as well as an insight into the real workings of her society.

Editorial Policy for these Texts and Translations

The *Epistre de la prison de vie humaine*—or to give its full title, *L'Epistre de la prison de vie humaine et d'avoir reconfort de morts d'amis et patience en adversité*—has survived in only one manuscript, French 24786 of the Bibliothèque Nationale in Paris. The present edition is based on an examination of this manuscript and a microfilm of it. The manuscript contains 97 folios on parchment, 170 × 120 millimeters, and is bound in red leather, bearing the arms of the Cardinal Richelieu. The manuscript formerly bore the number 1418 of the Sorbonne. On folio 97 recto, two former owners of the manuscript have written their names; one handwriting from the fifteenth century reads; "Ce livre est a moy, Berthemy Dusays"; the other from the sixteenth century: "Est a moy, De Tournon." The book then became the property of the Cardinal Richelieu. A more modern handwriting (probably from the nineteenth century) reads on the first folio: "This manuscript of the year 1417 contains a dialogue between reason and a chevalier on the difference between the present life and that enjoyed by those who are dead in the grace of God."

Two texts are included in the volume: the first a poem in the form of a dialogue between Reason and a Knight, which runs from folio 5r to folio 34r. Each of the 156 stanzas is 8 verses long. The second text is *L'Epistre de la prison*, which is dated by her as being finished on January 20, 1417. *L'Epistre de la prison* runs from folio 36r to folio 97r. The text is divided into 13 unnumbered chapters, the titles of which, as well as the title proper of the text, have rubrics. There are no miniatures, but all capitals of each chapter are colored in blue, red, and gold. The first folio containing the text has an inner margin of a green, red, and gold "ivy-leaf" work, and occupying the upper part of the folio is the large number "174." The text is written by a single hand, with one column to the page and 18 lines per page. It is foliated in Roman numerals in a cursive hand, clearly later than that of the copyist. Two further remarks might be made on the text. The punctuation is erratic: sometimes there is a space between two semantic or breath groups, sometimes a dot, and at other times, a slash. A number of common abbreviations have been used.

The current edition makes the following modifications: *i* and *u* used as consonants have been changed to *j* and *v*. We have used the cedilla and the apostrophe according to modern French usage, as well as modern French punctuation and capitals. The tonic *e* has been marked with an acute accent, and at times it has been used to distinguish between two words which would otherwise read as homographs. The tréma has been used to mark a hiatus as it would be read in modern French. The need for emendations has been very rarely necessary. The same editing principles have been used for the other two epistles. The text of the *Lamentacion sur les maux de la guerre civile*, found in only one manuscript, B.N. French 24864, is based on the edition done by Thomassy in 1838. A few corrections have been introduced. The *Epistre a la royne* can be found in several manuscripts: B.N. French 580(A), 604(B), 605(C), and Oxford, All Souls MS 182. The text presented in this volume is based on the 1838 Thomassy edition of 580(A), the only manuscript containing the *rondeau*. The sigla used are those used by M. D. Legge in her 1941 edition of the text, which was based on All Souls MS 182.

Acknowledgments

I wish to express my gratitude to Professor James J. Wilhelm for putting his time and erudition at my disposal to guide me through this edition. I am also indebted to George Wolf for his valuable suggestions, and to Dr. Carol Lanham, who encouraged me in my research. A special word of thanks is due to Jacqueline Simon for her reading of the manuscript, and especially to Elizabeth Richardson, whose editing and typing talents are deeply appreciated. Finally, my gratitude goes to Jon Wisman, who shared my great enthusiasm for the writings of Christine de Pizan.

The American University   J.A.W.
Washington, D.C

Select Bibliography

I. The Works of Christine de Pizan

A. *Modern Editions*

Lavision-Christine. Ed. Mary Louis Towner. Washington, D.C.: The Catholic University of America Press, 1932.

Ditié de la pucelle. Ed. Josette A. Wisman in "L'Humanisme dans l'oeuvre de Christine de Pisan." Diss. The Catholic University of America, 1976. Also in Angus J. Kennedy and Kenneth Varty, "Christine de Pisan's *Ditié de Jehanne d'Arc*," *Nottingham Medieval Studies 18* (1974), 29–55; *19* (1975), 53–76.

L'Epistre d'Othea. Ed. Halina D. Loukipoulos in "Classical Mythology in the Works of Christine de Pisan, with an Edition of *L'Epistre Othea* from the Manuscript Harley 4431." Diss. University of Michigan, 1977.

Epistres sur le Roman de la Rose. Ed. Eric Hicks in *Le Débat sur "Le Roman de la Rose."* Paris: Champion, 1977.

Epistre à Isabelle de Bavière, Reine de France, in Raymond Thomassy: *Essai sur les écrits politiques de Christine de Pisan, suivi d'une notice littéraire et de pièces inédites.* Paris: Debécourt, 1838. Also in Mary D. Legge: *Anglo-Norman Letters and Petitions from All Souls Manuscript 182.* Oxford: Blackwell, 1941.

Lamentacion sur les maux de la Guerre civile, in Raymond Thomassy: *Essai sur les écrits politiques de Christine de Pisan, suivi d'une notice littéraire et de pièces inédites.* Paris: Debécourt, 1838.

Le Livre du chemin de lonc estude. Ed. Robert Puschell. Berlin: s.l. 1887. Also in Patricia B. Eargle, "An Edition of Christine de Pisan's *Livre du chemin de lonc estude*." Diss. University of Georgia, 1973.

Le Livre de la cité des Dames. Ed. Maureen Curnow in "An Edition of Christine de Pisan's *Le Livre de la cité des Dames.*" Diss. Vanderbilt University, 1975.

Le Livre du corps de policie. Ed. Robert H. Lucas. Geneva: Droz, 1967.

Le Livre des fais et bonnes meurs du sage Roy, Charles V. Ed. Suzanne Solente. 2 vols. Paris: Champion, 1936–1941.

Le Livre de la mutacion de Fortune. Ed. Suzanne Solente. 4 vols. Paris: A. et J. Picard: 1959.

Le Livre de la paix. Ed. Charity C. Willard. The Hague: Mouton, 1958.

Le Livre des trois vertus. Ed. Lore L. Debower in "*Le Livre des Trois Vertus* of Christine de Pisan." Diss. University of Massachusetts, 1978.

Oeuvres poétiques. Ed. Maurice Roy. 3 vols. Paris: Didot et Co., 1886–1896.

Les sept psaumes allegorisés. Ed. Ruth R. Rains. Washington, D.C.: The Catholic University of America Press, 1965.

B. Translations

L'Epistre d'Othea. Two English translations were made in the fifteenth century, one by Stephen Scrope, and the other by Anthony Babyngton. The Scrope translation was edited by George F. Warner: London: Roxburghe Club, 1904, and Curt F. Bühler: London: Univ. Press, 1970. The Babyngton translation was edited by James D. Gordon: Philadelphia: The Univ. of Pennsylvania Press, 1942. In 1540, Robert Wyer translated and printed the text.

Le Livre de la cité des Dames. The fifteenth-century Dutch translation *Stede der Vrouwen* can be found in B.L., MS Add. 20698. In 1521, Brian Anslay published his *Boke of the Cyte of Ladyes*, printed by Henry Pepwell. A modern English translation was done by Earl Jeffrey Richards: *The Book of the City of Ladies.* New York: Persea Books, 1982.

Le Livre des fais d'armes et de chevalerie. Translated and printed by William Caxton in 1490, edited by A.T.P. Byles: London: Oxford Univ. Press, 1932.

Le Livre des trois vertus. A Portuguese translation can be found in the National Library in Madrid in MS 11515. A printed edition of this text was made around 1518 under the title *Espelho de Christina.*

Le Livre du corps de policie. An English translation of this text exists in MS Kk. 15 in the Cambridge University Library. In 1521, John Skot printed a translation under the title *The Bodye of Polycye*, which was edited by Diane Bornstein in: *The Middle English Translation of Christine de Pisan's "Livre du corps de policie."* Heidelberg: Winter, 1977.

Proverbes Moraux. This work, edited by Maurice Roy in Vol. 3 of *Oeuvres Poétiques de Christine de Pisan*, was translated by Anthony Wydeville (Woodville), and printed by Caxton in 1478 under the title *The Morale Proverbes of Christyne.*

II. Critical Works

Bailly, Renée. "La bonne Dame de Pisan." *Mercure de France, 305* (1949), 563–70. A brief introduction to C.'s life, works, and milieu.

Batard, Yvonne. "Dante et Christine de Pisan (1364–1430)." In *Missions et Démarches de la Critique: Mélanges offerts au Professeur J. A. Vier.* Vol. II. Paris: Klincksieck, 1973, pp. 341–51. Believes that by using some of Dante's metaphors in the *Chemin de lonc estude* and the *Mutacion de Fortune*, C. de Pizan presented Dante to France for the first time.

Becker, Philip A. "Christine de Pisan." *Zeitschrift für französische Sprache und Literatur, 54* (1931), 129–64. A review article of Pinet's *Christine de Pisan* with corrections of Pinet's dates.

Bell, Susan G. "Christine de Pizan (1364–1430): Humanism and the Problems of a Studious Woman." *Feminist Studies, 3* (Spring-Summer 1976), 173–84. C's studious life led to a "painful estrangement from society."

Blum-Erhard, Anna. "Christine de Pisan. Eine Bahnbrecherin geistigen Frauensberufs." *Die Literatur Monatschrift für Literaturfreunde, 41* (1939), 540–43. An analysis of C.'s poetical works, with some translations into German.

Boivin le Cadet. "Vie de Christine de Pisan et de Thomas de Pisan son père." *Mémoires de l'Académie Royale des Inscriptions et Belles-Lettres, 2* (1736), 706–22. The first major study of C.'s life and some of her works.

Boldingh-Goemans, W. L. *Christine de Pizan, 1364–1430: Haar Tijd, haar Leven, haar Werken.* Rotterdam: Nijgh and Van Ditman, 1948.

An introduction in Dutch to C.'s time, life, and works; follows Pinet very closely.

Bornstein, Diane. "Humanism in Christine de Pisan's *Livre du corps de policie.*" *Les Bonnes Feuilles,* 3 (Fall, 1974), 100–15. Views this work more as a humanist document than a "conservative piece of chivalric idealism."

Bozzolo, Carla. "*Il Decameron* come fonte del *Livre de la cité des dames* di Christine de Pisan." In *Miscellanea di studi e richerche sul quattrocento francese.* Ed. Franco Simone. Torino: Giappichelli Editore, 1967; pp. 3–24. Some of C.'s sources for *Cité des dames* are Boccaccio's *Decameron* and *De mulieribus claris.*

Bruins, Jan G. *Observations sur la langue d'Eustache Deschamps et de Christine de Pisan.* Dordrecht: De dordrechtshe Drukkerij, 1925. Finds C.'s style more elegant than Deschamps', and points out some of C.'s neologisms. Deals more with grammar than with style.

Bühler, Curt F. "The *Fleurs de toutes vertus* and Christine de Pisan's *L'Epistre d'Othea.*" *Publications of the Modern Language Association,* 62 (1947), 32–44. Believes that C. used the French translation of the *Fiore* as a model for the form of the *Epistre.*

———. "The *Fleurs de toutes vertus.*" *Publications of the Modern Language Association,* 64 (1949), 600–01. The author explains that the correct title of this work is *Chapelet des Vertus.*

———. "Sir John Falstof's Manuscripts of the *Epistre d'Othéa* and Stephen Scrope's Translation of this Text." *Scriptorium,* 3 (1949), 123–28.

———. "Wirk Alle Thyng by Conseil." *Speculum,* 24 (1949), 412–13. The proverb: *Omnia fac cum consilio* is used by Chaucer and in C.'s *Epistre d'Othea.*

———. "Christine de Pisan and a Saying Attributed to Socrates." *Philological Quarterly,* 33 (1954), 418–20.

———. "The *Assembly of Gods* and Christine de Pisan." *English Language Notes,* 4 (1967), 251–54. The anonymous author of the *Assembly of Gods* may have been inspired by the *Epistre d'Othea.*

Bumgardner, George H. "Tradition and Modernity from 1380 to 1405: Christine de Pizan." Diss. Yale, 1970. Notes the Italian sources of C.

Campbell, P.G.C. *L'Epître d'Othéa: Etude sur les sources de Christine de Pisan.* Paris: Champion, 1924. Still the best study on the mss. and sources of C.'s *Epistre d'Othea.*

———. "Christine de Pisan en Angleterre." *Revue de Littérature Comparée*, 5 (1925), 659–70. The author examines the fortune of C.'s works in England and her literary influence on such writers as Hoccleve and William Worcester. The best article on the subject.

Chesney, Kathleen. "Two Manuscripts of Christine de Pisan." *Medium Aevum*, 1 (1932), 35–41. The two Oxford mss. contain the *Epistre d'Othea*.

Cigada, Sergio. "Christine de Pisan e la traduzione inglese della poesia di Charles d'Orléans." *Aevum*, 32 (1958), 507–17.

———. "Il tema arturiano del 'Chateau Tournant,' Chaucer et Christine de Pisan." *Studi Medievali*, 2 (1961), 576–606.

Du Castel, Françoise. *Ma Grand-mère Christine de Pizan*. Paris: Hachette, 1936.

———. *Damoiselle Christine de Pizan, veuve de Me Etienne de Castel, 1364–1431*. Paris: A. et J. Picard, 1972. The author says that she is a descendant of C. de Pisan. The 1972 book is an expanded version of the 1936 original. It is heavily and beautifully illustrated, and an excellent introduction to C. for the layman.

Duchemin, Henri. "Les sources du *Livre des fais et bonnes meurs du sage roi Charles V* de Christine de Pisan." *Positions des Thèses de l'Ecole des Chartes*, 1891.

Dulac, Liliane. "Christine de Pisan et le malheur des 'Vrais Amans.' " In *Mélanges de Langue et de Littérature Médiévales offerts à Pierre Le Gentil*. Paris: S.E.D.E.S., 1973, pp. 223–33.

———. "Un mythe didactique chez Christine de Pizan: Sémiramis ou la veuve héroïque." In *Mélanges de Philologie Romane offerts à Charles Camproux*. Montpellier: C.E.O., 1978, I, 315–43. Comparing Semiramis' story as told in several versions and C. de Pizan's, Dulac concludes that C.'s heroine is great only insofar as she identifies herself as a man.

Dupré, Alexandre. "Histoire de Charles V par Christine de Pisan." *Mélanges historiques et littéraires, la plupart concernant le pays blésois*. 6, s.a., 33–44.

Edmonds, Barbara P. "Aspects of Christine de Pisan's Social and Political Ideas." Diss. University of Maryland, 1972. A study of C.'s social and political thinking.

Favier, Marguerite. *Christine de Pisan, muse des cours souveraines*. Lausanne: Rencontres, 1967. A presentation of C.'s poetic works.

Finkel, Helen Ruth. "The Portrait of the Woman in the Works of Christine de Pisan." Diss. Rice Univ., 1972.

Flutre, L. F. "Eustache Deschamps et Christine de Pisan ont-ils utilisé *Les faits des Romains?*" *Cultura Neolatina, 13* (1953), 229–40. C. certainly used this anthology, as the critic proves in comparing it with the *Mutacion de Fortune.*

Gabriel, Astrik L. "The Educational Ideas of Christine de Pisan." *Journal of the History of Ideas, 16* (1955), 3–21. A sympathetic examination of C.'s teachings to her son, to women, and to all.

Gauvard, Claude. "Christine de Pisan a-t-elle eu une pensée politique? A propos d'ouvrages récents." *La Revue Historique, 508* (1973), 417–30. An extremely interesting article which analyzes C.'s political ideas through the dedications and contents of some of her works, and tries to place her first in the Orléans faction, then in Burgundy's.

Gay, Lucy M. "On the Language of Christine de Pisan." *Modern Philology, 6* (1908), 1–18. Still the best basic article on the subject.

Gompertz, Stéphane. "Le Voyage allégorique chez Christine de Pisan." *Voyage, Quête, Pélérinage, 522* (1979), 195–208.

Ignatius, Mary Ann. "A Look at the Feminism of Christine de Pizan." *Proceedings of the Pacific Northwest Conference on Foreign Languages, 29,* 2 (1978), 18–21.

Jeanroy, Alfred. "Boccace et Christine de Pisan, le *De claris mulieribus* principale source du *Livre de la cité des dames.*" *Romania, 48* (1922), 93–105.

Kastenberg, Mathilde. "Die Stellung der Frau in der Dichtungen der Christine de Pisan." Diss. University of Heidelberg, 1909.

Koch, Friedrich. *Leben und Werke der Christine de Pisan.* Leipzig: Goslar a. Harz, 1885.

Laigle, Mathilde. *"Le Livre des trois vertus" de Christine de Pisan et son milieu historique et littéraire.* Paris: Champion, 1912. The first lengthy study of *Le Livre des trois vertus.*

Lecoy, Félix. "Notes sur quelques ballades de Christine de Pisan." In *Mélanges de philologie française offerts à Robert Guiette.* Antwerp: De nederlandsche Boekhandel, 1961, pp. 107–114. Revises Roy and Pinet's recount of C.'s poems collected in mss. dated 1405–10.

Le Gentil, Pierre. "Christine de Pisan, poète méconnu." In *Mélanges d'histoire littéraire offerts à Daniel Mornet.* Paris: Nizet, 1959, pp. 1–10.

Liewens, Robrecht. "Kerstine van Pizan." *Spiegel der Letteren, 3* (1959), 1–15.

McLeod, Enid. *The Order of the Rose: The Life and Ideas of Christine de Pizan*. Ottowa: Rowan and Littlefield, 1976. A clear and eminently readable introduction.

Margolis, Nadia. "The Poetics of History: An Analysis of Christine de Pizan's *Livre de la Mutacion de Fortune*." Diss. Stanford, 1977.

———. "The Metamorphoses of Misery in the Poetry of Christine de Pizan, Charles d'Orléans, and François Villon." In *Fifteenth Century Studies*. Ed. Guy R. Mermier and Edelgard E. DuBruck. Ann Arbor: University Microfilms International. *1*, 185–92.

Minto, William. "Christine de Pisan, A Mediaeval Champion of Her Sex." *McMillan Magazine*, 20 March 1886, pp. 264–74. One of the first modern introductions to the English-speaking audience; a thorough, though sometimes erroneous, study of her life and works.

Mombello, Gianni. "Per una edizione critica dell'*Epistre Othea* di Christine de Pizan." *Studi Francesi, 24* (1964), 401–17.

———. "Notizia su due manoscritti contenenti *L'Epistre Othea* di Christine de Pizan ed altre opere non identificate." *Studi Francesi, 31* (1967), 1–23.

———. "La tradizione manoscritta dell' *Epistre Othea* di Christine de Pizan; prolegomeni all'edizione del testo." Diss. Torino, 1967. In these three articles, Mombello identifies forty-three manuscripts of *Othea*, and examines the four dedications of the work.

———. "J.-M.-L. Coupé e H. Walpole: Gli amori di Christine de Pizan." *Studi Francesi, 56* (1972) 5–25. Coupé—and not Walpole—was probably the first to write about the "love story" between C. and the Earl of Salisbury.

Moulin, Janine. *Christine de Pisan*. Paris: Seghers, 1962. A selection of her poetical works.

Müller, Ernst. *Zur Syntax der Christine de Pisan*. Greifswald: J. Abel, 1886. A short and rarely illuminating work on the subject.

Nicolini, Elena. "Christine de Pizzano (L'origine e il nome)." *Cultura Neolatina, 1* (1941), 143–50. Shows that Thomas de Pisan came from Pizzano, a small town near Bologna, and not from Pisa, as was previously believed.

Nys, Ernest. *Christine de Pisan et ses principales oeuvres*. The Hague:

Martinus Nijhoff, 1914. Thinks C.'s military works owe much to Honoré Bonnet's *L'Arbre des batailles*.

Pernoud, Régine. *Christine de Pisan*. Paris: Calmann-Lévy, 1982. An unscholarly and sympathetic presentation of C.

Piaget, Arthur. "Chronologie des Epistres sur le *Roman de la Rose*." In *Etudes romanes dédiées à Gaston Paris*. Paris: E. Bouillon, 1891, pp. 113–20.

Pinet, Marie-Josèphe. *Christine de Pisan, 1364–1430, étude biographique et littéraire*. Paris: Champion, 1927. Even if Pinet's book has been faulted for some inaccuracies, this lengthy study is still one of the best scholarly works on C.

Pugh, Annie R. "*Le Jugement du roy de Behaigne* de Guillaume de Machaut et *Le Dit de Poissy* de Christine de Pisan." *Romania*, 23 (1894), 1–86.

Reno, Christine. "Self and Society in *L'Avision-Christine* of Christine de Pisan." Diss. Yale Univ., 1972. A study of the role played by C. as an intellectual woman.

————. "Christine de Pisan's Use of the *Golden Legend* in the *Cité des dames*." *Les Bonnes Feuilles*, 3 (1974), 89–99.

Rice, J. P. "A Note on Christine de Pisan and Cecco d'Ascoli." *Italica*, 15 (1938), 145–151. In the *Cité des dames*, Christine makes a parallel between the two Italian astrologers, her father and Cecco d'Ascoli.

Richter, Bodo L. "A New Work by Christine de Pisan: *Les sept psaumes allegorisés*." *Studi Francesi*, 12 (1968), 68–73.

Rieger, Dietmar. "Die französische Dichterin im Mittelalter: Marie de France, die 'trobairitz,' Christine de Pizan." In *Die französische Autorin vom Mittelalter bis zur Gegenwart*. Wiesbaden: Bader und Fricke, 1979, pp. 1–45.

Robineau, E. M.-D. *Christine de Pisan, sa vie, ses oeuvres*. Saint-Omer: Fleury-Lemaire, 1882. Follows Boivin le Cadet very closely.

Rosier, Madeleine. "Christine de Pisan as a Moralist." Diss. Toronto, 1945.

Schaefer, Lucie. "Die Illustrationen zu den Handschriften der Christine de Pisan." *Marburger Jahrbuch für Kunstwissenschaft*, 10 (1937), 119–208. A presentation of the illustrations in C.'s manuscripts. Lists all the manuscripts containing illustrations.

Schilperort, Johanna C. "Guillaume de Machault et Christine de Pisan."

Diss. Univ. of Leyden, 1936. Finds that C.'s *Debat des deux amans* followed Machaut's *Jugement dou Roy de Navarre* in form and content. *Le Dit de Poissy* followed the *Jugement dou Roy de Behaigne.*

Schmidt, Albert Marie. "Christine de Pisan." *Revue des Sciences Humaines,* 122–23 (1962), 159–74. An unfinished article on the family of C., and the life that she may have lived in Paris.

Sims, Robert. "La Sincérité chez Christine de Pisan et Alain Chartier." *Chimères* (Fall 1976-Spring 1977), 39–48.

Solente, Suzanne. "Un traité inédit de Christine de Pisan, *L'Epistre de la prison de vie humaine.*" *Bibliothèque de l'Ecole des Chartes,* 85 (1924), 263–301. Solente describes the manuscript that she discovered at the B.N. An excellent and long introduction precedes the edition of excerpts of the text.

————. "Deux chapitres de l'influence littéraire de Christine de Pisan." *Bibliothèque de l'Ecole des Chartes,* 94 (1933), 27–43. A work entitled *Enseignements que une dame laisse a ses deulx filz en forme de testament,* and the *Louenge de mariage* by Pierre de Lesnauderie are very similar to some of C.'s works.

————. "Le *Jeu des Echecs moralisés,* source de la *Mutacion de Fortune.*" In *Recueil de travaux offert à M. Clovis Brunel.* Paris: Klincksieck, 1955, II, 556–65.

————. "Christine de Pisan," *Histoire littéraire de la France,* 40 (1969), 335–422. Recent scholarly treatment.

Temple, Maud E. "Christine de Pisan and the Victorine Revival." Diss. Radcliffe, 1912.

————. "Paraphrasing in the *Livre de Paix* of Christine de Pisan of the *Paradiso,* III-V." *Publications of the Modern Language Association,* 37 (1922), 182–86.

Thomassy, Raymond. *Essai sur les écrits politiques de Christine de Pisan, suivi d'une notice littéraire et de pièces inédites.* Paris: Debécourt, 1838. Contains the first edition of the *Lamentacion* and *Epistre a la royne.*

Toynbee, Paget. "Christine de Pisan and Sir John Maundeville." *Romania,* 21 (1892), 228–239. According to Toynbee, C., borrows heavily from Maundeville's *Travels* (1356) in the *Chemin de lonc estude.*

Wieland, Christoph Martin. "Christine de Pisan." *Deutscher Merkur,* 1 (1781), 200–29.

Wilkins, Nigel. "The Structure of Ballades, Rondeaux and Virelais in Froissart and in Christine de Pisan." *French Studies,* 23 (1969), 337–48.

Willard, Charity C. "The 'Three Virtues' of Christine de Pisan." *Boston Public Library Quarterly,* 2 (1950), 291–305. Describes Boston Public Library's MS 1528. The critic believes that *Le Livre des trois vertus* was a source of works by Chartier, Marche, and Marot.

———. "A Portuguese Translation of Christine de Pisan's *Livre des trois vertus.*" *Publications of the Modern Language Association,* 78 (1963), 459–64. The translation was done at the request of Queen Isabella of Portugal between 1447 and 1455.

———. "Christine de Pisan's Clock of Temperance." *L'Esprit Créateur,* 2 (1962), 149–54.

———. "An Autograph Manuscript of Christine de Pizan?" *Studi Francesi,* 9 (1965), 452–57. Believes that the rondeau written as a postscript to the *Epistre a la reine* in B.N. Fr. 580 was written by C. herself.

———. "The Manuscript Tradition of the *Livre des trois vertus* and Christine de Pisan's Audience." *Journal of the History of Ideas,* 27 (1966), 433–44.

———. "Christine de Pisan's Treatise on the Art of Warfare." In *Essays in Honour of Louis F. Solano.* Chapel Hill, 1970; pp. 179–91. One of C. de Pisan's sources for the *Livre des Fais d'armes et de chevalerie* was Petrarch.

Wisman, Josette A. "L'Humanisme dans l'oeuvre de Christine de Pisan." Diss. Catholic University, 1976.

———. "L'Eveil du sentiment national au Moyen Age: la pensée politique de Christine de Pisan." *La Revue Historique,* 522 (April-June 1977), 289–97.

———. "Manuscrits et Editions des oeuvres de Christine de Pisan." *Manuscripta,* 21 (1977), 144–53.

Woledge, Brian. "Le Thème de la pauvreté dans la *Mutacion de Fortune* de Christine de Pisan." In *La Fin du Moyen Age et Renaissance: Mélanges de philologie française offerts à Robert Guiette.* Antwerp: De Nederlandsche Boekhandel, 1961, pp. 97–106.

III. Study Aids

Anciennes Chroniques d'Angleterre par Jehan de Wavrin. Ed. Mlle Dupont. 3 vols. Paris, Librarie Renouard, 1863.

Calmette, Joseph. *Charles V.* Paris: Arthème Fayard, 1945.

Cartellieri, Otto. *The Court of Burgundy.* Trans. Malcolm Letts. New York: Barnes et Nobles, 1972.

Chronique d'Enguerrand de Monstrelet. Ed. L. Douët d'Arcq. 4 vols. Paris: Renouard, 1857.

Chronique de Jean Le Fèvre. Ed. François Morand. 2 vols. Paris: Librairie Renouard, 1881.

Chronique du religieux de St. Denys. Ed. L. Bellaguet. Paris: Crapelet, 1839–52.

Coville, Alfred, *Les premiers Valois et la guerre de cent ans.* Vol. IV of *Histoire de France illustrée.* Ed. Ernest Lavisse. Paris: Hachette, 1911.

————. *Gontier et Pierre Col et l'humanisme en France au temps de Charles VI.* Paris: Droz, 1934.

Delisle, Charles. *Recherches sur la librairie de Charles V, roi de France, 1337–1380.* 2 vols. 2nd ed., 1907. Amsterdam: Van Heusden, 1967.

Doutrepont, Georges. *La Littérature française à la cour des ducs de Bourgogne.* Paris: Champion, 1909.

Dow, Blanche Hinman. *The Varying Attitude Toward Women in French Literature of the Fifteenth Century: The Opening Years.* New York: Institute of French Studies, 1936.

Drinkwater, Geneva. "French Libraries in the Fourteenth and Fifteenth Centuries." In *The Medieval Library.* Ed. James W. Thompson. New York and London: Hafner, 1965, pp. 414–52.

Farinelli, Arturo. *Dante e la Francia dall'età media al secolo di Voltaire.* 2 vols. Milano: Hoepli, 1908.

Foulet, Lucien. "La Querelle du *Roman de la Rose.*" In *Histoire de la littérature française.* Ed. J. Bédier and P. Hazard. Paris: Larousse, 1923–24; II, 98–99.

Fowler, Kenneth. *The Age of Plantagenet and Valois: The Struggle for Supremacy, 1328–1498.* New York: Putnam, 1967.

Franklin, Alfred. *Les anciennes Bibliothèques de Paris.* 3 vols. Paris: Impériale, 1867–1873.

Henrici Quinti Angliae regis gesta. Ed. B. Williams. London: n.p. 1850.

Hentsch, Alice A. "De la littérature didactique au Moyen Age s'adressant spécialement aux femmes." Diss. Halle a. S., 1903.

Hibbert, Christopher. *Agincourt.* Philadelphia: Dufour, 1964.

Hicks, Eric. *Le Débat sur le Roman de la Rose.* Paris: Champion, 1977.

Histoire de Charles VI par Jean Jouvenal des Ursins. Ed. Denys Godefroy. Paris: Royale, 1653.

Jarrett, Bede. *Social Theories of the Middle Ages, 1200–1500.* Boston: Little, Brown & Co., 1926.

Kéralio, Louise de. *Collection des meilleurs ouvrages composés par des femmes.* 3 vols. Paris: Lagrange, 1787.

Kirkland, Dorothy. "France." In *Nationalism in the Middle Ages.* Ed. Charles L. Tipton. New York: Holt, Rinehart & Winston, 1972, pp. 80–92.

Lehmann, Andrée. *Le Rôle de la femme dans l'histoire de France au Moyen Age.* Paris: Berger-Levrault, 1952.

Meiss, Millard. *French Painting in the Time of Jean de Berry.* 2 vols. New York: Georges Braziller Inc. 1974.

Mollat, Michel. *Génèse médiévale de la France moderne.* Paris: Arthaud, 1970.

Monfrin, Jacques. "Humanisme et traductions au Moyen Age." In *L'Humanisme médiéval dans les littératures romanes du XIIᵉ au XIVᵉ siècle.* Ed. Anthime Fourrier. Paris: Klincksieck, 1964, pp. 217–46.

Nicolas, Sir K. H. *History of the Battle of Agincourt.* 2nd ed., 1832. Repr. New York: Barnes and Noble, 1970.

Patch, Howard Rollin. *The Goddess Fortuna in Mediaeval Literature.* Cambridge: Harvard, 1927.

———. *The Tradition of Boethius.* 2nd ed., 1935. New York: Russel & Russel, 1970.

Perroy, Edouard. *La Guerre de cent ans.* 2nd ed., 1945. Paris: Gallimard, 1976.

Poetical Works of Alain Chartier. Ed. J. C. Laidlaw. London: Cambridge Univ., 1974.

Richardson, Lula. *The Forerunners of Feminism in French Literature of the Renaissance.* Baltimore: Johns Hopkins, 1929.

Seward, Desmond. *The Hundred Years War: The English in France, 1337–1453.* New York: Atheneum, 1978.

Siciliano, Italo. *François Villon et les thèmes poétiques du Moyen Age.* 2nd ed. 1937. Paris: Nizet, 1967.

Simone, Franco. "La Présence de Boccace dans la culture française du XVᵉ siècle." *Journal of Medieval and Renaissance Studies,* 1 (1971), 17–32.

Thorndike, Lynn. *Science and Thought in the Fifteenth Century; Studies in the History of Medicine and Surgery, Natural and Mathematical Science, Philosophy, and Politics.* 8 vols. New York: Hafner, 1923–1958.

Titi Livii Foro-Juliensis Vita Henrici Quinti. Ed. T. Hearne. Oxford: Univ. Press, 1911.

Toffanin, Guiseppe. *History of Humanism.* Trans. Elio Gianturco. New York: Las Americas, 1954.

Vaughan, Richard. *John the Fearless.* New York: Barnes & Noble, 1966.

The Wheel of Fortune, a recurrent figure in Christine de Pizan's writings. From Gregor Reisch, *Margarita Philosophica*, 1503, Vol. 2, signature A7 verso. (Courtesy of Folger Shakespeare Library)

The Epistle of the
Prison of Human Life

Pour aucunement trouver remede et medicine a la griefve
maladie et enfermeté d'amertume de cuer et tristece de
pensee, par quoy flus de lermes--le quel a l'ame a tel cause   5
ne puet prouffiter, ne au corps valoir--peust estre restraint
et remis qui tant a couru et encores, dont c'est pitié, ne
cesse entre meismement les roynes, princesses, baronnesses,
dames, damoiselles du noble sang royal de France et
generalment le plus des femmes d'onneur frappees de ceste   10
pestillence en cestui françois royaume, a cause tant de
diverses mors ou prises de leurs prouchains, si comme maris,
enfans, freres, oncles, cousins, affins et amis; les uns
deffunts par bataille, les autres trespassez naturelment en
leurs lis, comme de maintes pertes et autres diverses   15
infortunes et aventures obliquement puis un temps survenues;
aviser comment se aucune chose proposer et ramener a memoire
porroit servir et estre valable a aucun reconfort, dont du
quel nombre des adoulees a ceste cause, redoubtee princesse,
ma Dame Marie de Berry, Duchesse de Bourbon et d'Auvergne,tu   20
n'as pas--dont il me poise--esté, ne n'es exempte ne
exceptee; et pour tant comme les merites de ta large charité
a moy estendue en cestui temps d'affliction presente ou amis
sont faillis aient esté a mon petit estat vesval aidier a
gouverner singulier secours--Dieu, par sa grace, retribueur   25
t'en soit--comme de ce et d'autres tes bienfais recongnoissant et non ingrate, desireuse d'en aucune chose comme
obligiee te povoir servir, a toy premierement des princesses
de ce dit royaume, quoyque par mouvement d'autre en feusse
chargee, sera adreciee ceste mienne epistre, qui, semblable- 30
ment et par consequant puist estre valable a toutes les
autres encheues es susdittes doleurs.
     Donques, haute princesse, je, ton humble servant, meu
de pitié et de loyale et vraie affection, comme dés pieça

*Here begins the epistle on the prison of human life and
how to find comfort with the death of friends and patience in
adversity.*

In order somehow to find a remedy and a cure for the
severe malady and infirmity caused by a bitter heart and sad   5
thoughts, a remedy which might restrain and dry up a flood of
tears that can benefit neither the soul nor be of value to
the body, and that has run and runs still--which is a pity--
even among the queens, princesses, baronesses, ladies and
young girls of the noble royal blood of France, and in   10
general among most of the ladies-in-waiting, who have been
stricken by this pestilence in this French kingdom: because
of so many various deaths and abductions of kin--husbands,
sons, brothers, uncles, cousins, relatives and friends, some
killed in battles, others passing away naturally in their   15
beds--and of so many losses and other various misfortunes
and adventures which have occurred unexpectedly for some
time; in order also to see if recalling anything to mind can
be of help and be of use in consolation, since among the
many ladies afflicted by this, Revered Princess, my Lady   20
Mary of Berry, Duchess of Bourbon and Auvergne,[1] you have not
been--so it seems to me--exempt or excepted; and therefore,
because the merits of your great charity, extended to me in
this present time of affliction when friends are missing,
have been helpful to my humble widowed state in providing a   25
personal assistance--may God, by His grace, reward you for
it!--and because I recognize and am not ungrateful for all
this and other good deeds of yours, and wishing to be able to
help you in anything, to you first of all among the princesses of this kingdom, this epistle of mine will be   30
addressed--although someone else has commissioned it--and it
consequently can also be of value to all who have fallen in
the aforementioned sufferings.
    Therefore, High Princess, because I, your humble
servant, moved by pity and loyal and true affection, began   35

[1]Mary (1375-1434) married three times: Louis of
Chatillon (d.1391) in 1386; Philip of Artois (d.1397) in
1393; and John of Bourbon (d.1434) in 1400.

3

ceste present oeuvre je eusse encommenciee, dont l'excusacion de plus tost n'avoir achevé diray en la fin, mais comme
mieux vaille tart que jamais et qu'encores ne soit, dont il
me poise, si comme sont faucilles aprés aoust, veu la male
disposicion du temps qui adés continue--Dieu, par sa grace, y   5
vueille brief remedier--m'y suis reprise en entencion de, par
la Dieu grace, la traire a bonne fin; et pour ce qu'achoison
de mort d'amis qui souvent advient est la principal douleur
qui ait grevé les cuers des loyales dames bien amantes, comme
ce soit chose inrecouvrable et fort a oublier, sera le   10
fondement de ceste mienne epistre prise sur celle matiere en
donnant reconfort.

   Et pour tant en ta personne qui bien en a eue sa part,
je parleray a toutes semblablement, en faisant mon devoir,
par moien d'escripture, selon mon petit savoir et   15
congnoissance, de te ramentevoir aucunes raisons a propos
prises et puisiees tant en hystoires approuvees comme es
Saintes Escriptures, qui te pevent et doivent mouvoir a
restraindre et delaissier l'effusion de lermes qui par grant
douleur souvent habondent sur ta face, a cause de la perte de 20
la chevalerie françoise et pour la grant quantité des trés
nobles et dignes princes royaulx de France, si prouchains et
affins de ton sang, que mors ou pris comme mary, filz, pere,
cousins germains, que ducs, que contes, et tant haute gent,
t'en trouver seule et desnuee; quoyque, la Dieu grace, tous   25
sans reprouche, ains trés honnorablement, des trespassez:
les uns naturelment comme catholiques en fin glorieuse et
congnoissance de leur Createur, trés crestiennement et en
grant humilité; les autres contre les ennemis anglois,
assaillans d'une part, et eulx deffendeurs de l'autre, avec   30
les martirs de Dieu esleus en la juste deffense par bataille,
fais obeissans jusques a la mort pour justice soustenir et le
droit de la couronne françoise et leur souverain seigneur,
des quelz et pour les quelz et leurs semblables, dit
l'Euvangille: "Beneurez sont ceulx qui seuffrent pour   35
justice"; et trés noble et redoubtee Dame, avant que plus
oultre je procede en ceste matiere, suppli humblement ton
humaine debonnaireté, que n'ait a mal se en singulier je

4

this work a long time ago (and I will tell at the end the
reason why I did not finish it earlier, but since late is
better than never, or so it seems to me that it is, just
like scythes after August, considering the unfortunate
disposition of the time which continues--may God, by His   5
grace, remedy it quickly!--), I have gone back to the task,
intending with the grace of God to draw it to an end; and
because the death of friends which has been occurring frequently is the main sorrow which has grieved the hearts of
loyal and loving ladies, and since this is a thing from   10
which one cannot recover and which is hard to forget, the
foundation of my epistle will be set upon this subject,
while giving comfort.

　　And yet through you, who have had to bear your share
[of grief], I shall speak to all ladies alike, in doing my   15
duty by means of the written word, in so far as my meager
wisdom and knowledge are able, in calling to mind the
reasons culled, as the occasion called for, from accepted
stories as from the Holy Scriptures; and these can and
should restrain and stop the effusion of tears which, in   20
your great grief flow often on your face, because of the
loss of French chivalry, and for the great number of very
noble and worthy royal princes of France, so close and akin
to your blood, dead or captive, such as husbands, sons
fathers, first cousins, or dukes, counts, and so many high   25
persons of whom you find yourself deprived and devoid;[2]
although all of the deceased, by the grace of God, died
beyond reproach and honorably--some naturally as Catholics
in a glorious end and in knowledge of their Creator, in a
very Christian manner and in great humility; others, attack-   30
ing the English enemies on one side, and resisting on the
other as just defenders, were elected with God's martyrs
through battle, and were made obedient until death to sustain justice and the right of the French crown and their
sovereign Lord; of them and for them and their fellowmen the   35
Gospel says:　"Blessed be those who suffer for justice";[3]
and, Noble and Revered Lady, before I go any further in this
matter, I humbly beg your Goodness not to think badly of me

[2]Mary's husband, John of Bourbon, and her son by her
second marriage, Charles of Artois, were taken prisoners by
the English.　John died in England in 1434; Charles was
released in 1438.　John of Berry, Mary's father, died on
June 15, 1416.　Mary's cousins, Charles of Albret, Anthony
of Burgundy, and Philip of Nevers, were killed at Agincourt.
Another cousin, John of Harcourt, was also taken prisoner.
[3]*Matthew* 5.10.

parle a toy, c'est assavoir par tu, ainsi comme meismement
autrefois ay parlé en mes petites escriptures et epistres a
ton trés noble pere, l'excellent duc de Berry--dont l'ame
soit au ciel--et a maints autres princes et princesses,
suivant le stille en ceste partie des poëtes et orateurs.   5

A mon premier propos, trés noble Dame, pour ce que les
paroles dittes et venues de moy pourroient estre de trop
petite efficace au regart de ta grant douleur, en te de-
moustrant et ramentevant matiere de pacience, te plaise au
fort vouloir adjouster foy a la Sainte Escripture et a ce que   10
les glorieux dotteurs et maints sages atteurs ont dit, tant
d'avoir pacience es choses adverses que Fortune livre par
diverses aventures, comme de la gloire et beneurté de ceulx
qui meurent en grace, entre les quelz bien mors, ma trés
redoubtee Dame, povons, par les signes catholiques et vraies   15
conjettures qui de ce nous ont fait demoustrance, comprendre
ceulx dessusdis, les quelz nature et pitié filiale et fra-
ternelle te fait tant plaindre; pour la quel chose te puis
faire une tel question et demande, c'est assavoir, le quel
party plus tost esliroies: ou que yceulx feussent encore au   20
monde vivans et estre y deussent, tant comme tu vivras ou
assez plus, mais neantmoins feust telle l'aventure ou la
destinee qu'emprisonnez tout leur vivant demourassent en
peril de mort par chascun jour, usant leur vie en divers
travaulx, perilz, dangiers et cuisençons; ou qu'il feust   25
ainsi que un chascun d'eulx feust esleu estre empereur d'un
tel monde que cestui est, et possible feust que jamais ne
mourussent, ains a tousjours vesquissent en toute prosperité,
seingneurie, joye, transquilité, et paix? Certes, ma Dame,
je ne doubte pas que plus chier aroies ce que pour toy   30
meismes tu esliroies: c'est a savoir le derrain des susdis
.ii. partis. O redoubtee Dame, ne croirons-nous donques les
Saintes Escriptures et la foy de Dieu vraie, sans la quelle
avoir et tenir fermement, nul ne puet plaire a Dieu n'estre
sauvé, si comme dit Saint Paul?   35

Et pour tant a propos dit Saint Bernart, que ceste vie
mortele puet estre a un chascun figuree a la prison, car tout
ainsi que la closture de la prison detient le prisonnier, si
a destroit que user ne puet de ses mesmes vouloirs, n'acom-
plir ses desirs, ains communement a tout le contraire,   40
semblablement, l'ame raisonnable, qui la plus noble partie
est de l'omme, sans la quelle le corps n'est fors terre et
pourreture, est detenue emprisonnee et liee dedens le corps
tant comme elle y est, voire si contrainte et empeschiee par

36. Bernardus *in margin*

6

if I speak to you in the singular, that is by *tu*, just as I
once spoke in my little writings and epistles to your very
noble father, the excellent Duke of Berry--in Heaven rest
his soul--and to many other princes and princesses, following
in this the style of poets and orators.   5

  As to my first subject, Very Noble Lady, since my own
words may be of little consequence with respect to your great
sorrow, in showing you and calling to mind matters of
patience, may it please you to give credence to the Holy
Scriptures and to what the glorious doctors and many wise   10
authors have written: as much concerning having patience in
the adversities that Fortune doles out by means of various
vicissitudes, as concerning the glory and the blessedness of
those who die in grace; and among those who died well, my
Very Revered Lady, we can, through the Catholic signs and the   15
true manifestations which have shown this to us, include all
those aforementioned men, for whom nature and filial and
fraternal love make you grieve so; for this reason, I may
ask you the following question and request, that is, which
course would you choose: should those men still be alive in   20
this world as long as you live or even longer, yet such
should be their fate that they should remain imprisoned for
the rest of their lives in deadly peril every day, wearing
out their lives in various labors, perils, dangers, and torments; or should each of them be elected emperor of such a   25
world as this, and possibly should never die, rather should
live in total prosperity, power, joy, tranquility, and
peace? Indeed, my Lady, I do not doubt that you would
prefer the course that you would select for yourself: that
is the second of the two. Oh, Revered Lady, shall we not   30
believe the Holy Scriptures and have and firmly uphold the
true faith of God, without which no one can be favored by
God nor be saved, as Saint Paul says?[4]

  And on that subject, Saint Bernard said that this mortal
life can be, for all of us, compared to a prison,[5] for just   35
as the enclosure of a prison detains the prisoner so tightly
that he cannot make use of his very intentions nor fulfill
his desires, rather, he ordinarily experiences the opposite,
in the same manner, the reasonable soul, which is the
noblest part of man, without which the body is only earth   40
and rot, is kept prisoner and bound inside the body as long
as it is in it, and is even so constrained and prevented by
the weight and the thickness of the said vessel, that it
does not have the power, except in a very small way, to

[4]*Hebrews* 11.6. [5]St. Bernard, *De virtute oboedientiae,
et septem ejus gradidus.*

7

la pesanteur et rudece du dit vaissel, qu'elle n'a povoir,
fors en bien petite partie, d'user de ses propres inclina-
cions et vouloirs, ains lui convient obeir le plus des fois
tout au contraire de la ou elle tent. Et pour tant, bien
dit a propos le sage Helbertus: que quant l'omme muert,   5
l'ame est desliee et desprisonnee. Donques est-il ainsi que
tout homme vivant en ce mortel monde--comme tous egaulx
soions, grans, moiens et petis--quant en ceste qualité se
puet et doit reputer prisonnier, or est a veoir se en celle
prison homme de quelque estat qu'il soit, demeure asseur du   10
tout aise et sans peril. O, com grant bien fust avoir
seigneurie, puissance, prinsee, richesces, et bon les feist
acquerre se par telz moiens peussent estre evitez et
eschevez les mortelz perilz et divers agais de la faulse
Fortune et les griefs cuisençons et tant penibles travaulx   15
que le monde livre! Mais, se grandeurs mondanes y pevent
servir ou non, assez d'exemples le nous aprennent, et sont a
savoir si comme quoy.

   Hé, que valu au grant empereur Alixandre sa haute
puissance soubz la quel main tout le monde trembloit? Lui   20
fut-elle donques garent lors que les traitres et ses meismes
servans en petit de heure le getterent mort par poisons? Pou
lui dura la joye de la fin de son grant travail a la con-
queste du monde que il ne posseda pas .iii. jours entiers.
Mais que dirons-nous de Julius Cesar? Ot-il bien emploié ses   25
paines quant, par si longs travaux, tant de perilz passez, de
bleceures souffertes et mesaises en pluseurs et diverses
batailles, conquit la plus grant partie du monde? Lors que
Fortune l'ot assis au plus hault de sa roe et quant repos
cuida seignourir en triumphe comme empereur, o, comment a   30
paines cuidast-il que homme lui osast nuire ne a pou meismement Fortune, cil qui de tant de perilz fu eschappez? Mais
ne fut-il en pou d'eure occis de greffes entre ses barons en
son privé conseil meismes par ses citoïens? Item, le bon
prince Pompee en ot-il moins? Mais fut-il onques nul   35
meilleur de lui en toutes chevalereuses graces et meurs
vertueux, si que devisent les hystoires rommaines, qui tout
Orient ot conquis et les pors et passages de mer despeschiez
de larrons et tous conquis? Mais qu'en ot-il enfin, a nom
Dieu? Le chef trenchié par les mains de traitres a qui il   40
avoit bien fait. O, main de traitre et entencion traitreuse,
tu soies maudite! Tant de maulx sont venus a ton occasion!
Ha, tant de bons as desavanciez, dont qui tout vouldroit
dire, seroit longue arenge!

   5. Albertus *in margin*

exercise its own inclinations and desires, and instead it
has to follow most of the time the opposite of its own ten-
dency. And on that subject, the wise Albert speaks very
much to the purpose: when a man dies, his soul is delivered
and set free.[6] Thus each man alive in this mortal world--   5
since we are all equal: high, middle, and low--in so far as
he is in this condition, can and must consider himself a
prisoner; however, it remains to be seen if, in this prison,
man of any position whatsoever remains assured of all comfort, and of no peril. Oh, how good it could be to have   10
control, power, fame, wealth, and how good it would be to
have acquired them, if in so doing, the mortal perils, the
various dangers of false Fortune, the deep torments, and so
many painful labors handed out by this world could be avoided
and shunned! But, whether worldly achievements can be of   15
use or not, many examples tell it to us, and they are as
follows.

    Ah! Of what value was his strong power to the great
emperor Alexander under which everyone trembled? Did it
protect him when the traitors and his own servants quickly   20
murdered him by using poison? Short was his joy at the end
of his great venture, the conquest of the world which he did
not own for a full three days. And what shall we say of
Julius Caesar? Did he put his pains to good use when, after
having gone through so many labors, so many perils, after   25
having suffered wounds and injuries in many and various
battles, he conquered the greatest part of the world? When
Fortune placed him at the top of her wheel, and, when rested,
he planned to rule triumphantly as emperor, how could he
even think that someone or Fortune herself would dare to harm   30
him, he who had escaped so many perils? But did he not die
of stab-wounds inflicted by his citizens in his very privy
council and among his barons? Similarly, did the good
prince Pompey not get less? Was there never anyone better
than he in respect to knightly qualities and virtuous habits,   35
as the Roman histories say, who had conquered all of the
Orient and made the harbors and sea passages free of pirates,
and conquered everyone? But what did he get at the end,
dear God? His head was cut off by the hands of the traitors
whom he had treated well. Oh, hand of a traitor and   40
treacherous scheme, be damned! So many evils have happened
on your account! Ah, you have ruined so many good men,
the list of whom, if anyone wanted to tell it all, would be
long!

    [6]Albertus Magnus, *De arte moriendi*.

La Prison de Vie Humaine

Mais je ne fais pas doubte qu'avec Judas ne soit de telz
a la parfin dure la punicion, comme Dieu soit juste. Semblablement, Scipion l'Auffriquan, le preux chevalier qui tant ot
fait de biens et toute Auffrique et la grant cité de Cartage
et auques toutes les Espaignes conquis aux Rommains par   5
merveilleux travaulx et vaillantise d'armes, mais quelle en
fut la fin? Ne morut-il povre et exillié? Ha, monde, est-ce
donques grant joye et tout gaingnie que de regner en toy?
Et certes, qui le mieulx te sert a souvent le pire loyer et
si n'est mie sans paine.   10
   A brief dire, infinis exemples pourroie ramentevoir des
divers perilz et dures aventures qui tousjours aviennent en
ceste susdite dolereuse prison de vie humaine. Et, qui plus
est et fait a noter, tout ainsi que quant il fait orage de
temps et que les tempestes courans par l'air, menees par   15
divers vens, plus tost encontrent et debatent les sommetons
et combles des hautes tours et souvent les trebuchent
qu'elles ne font les bas et moiens estages, semblablement,
les soufflemens de Fortune, quant elle est contraire, plus
perilleusement s'embat sur les hautes personnes que sur les   20
moïennes ou basses. Et pour ce, dit Boece en son secont
livre, que plus prouffite la male Fortune que la propre, car
la bonne avugle par ses prosperitez et fait croire estat
seur, et la perverse fait appercevoir la verité de sa
muableté et que fier on ne s'y doit.   25

Cy devise des mauvais cruelz et comment sont punis
meismement en ce monde.

Au propos dessus dit, se les perilz sont grans meismes
aux bons et aux trés vertueux et n'en sont exemps tout
aient-ilz fait maints biens, comme Dieu le consente aucune   30
fois pour leur purgacion en cestui monde, ou a l'accroissement de leur merite par pacience si que dit Saint Augustin,
certes ne doivent pas estre asseur, ains bien trembler et
avoir paour les felons detestables, mauvais, plains de venin
et de faulse ambicion, persecuteurs et destruiseurs de   35
nature humaine, insaciables de respandre sang et de tout mal
faire, dont en la religion cristienne en y a au jour d'ui
de telz plus que onques—mais dont c'est grant pitié—et qui
pis est, meismement de telz qui n'espargnent, ne n'ont
regart a parenté, affinité, ne autre congnoissance. O, gent   40
avuglee, gent mescongnoissant et hors la loy de Dieu! Ceulx
qui ce font, n'ont-ilz avis comment la vie de ce monde est

But I do not doubt that, as with Judas, the punishment of such men will be harsh at the very end, since God is just. Similarly, Scipio the African, the stalwart knight who did so much good, conquered from the Romans all of Africa, the great city of Carthage and even all the realms of Spain by marvelous efforts and boldness of arms--what was his end? Did he not die poor and exiled? Ah, world, is it truly great joy and all gain to rule over you? Indeed, he who serves you the best often has the worst reward, and it is not without pain!

In brief, I could recall many examples of various perils and terrible events which always occur in the aforesaid prison of human life. Moreover and most importantly, just as when there is a storm, and the tempests running through the air, pushed by various winds, encounter and hit the tops and lofts of the high towers, often knocking them down more readily than they would knock the low and middle stories, similarly, the blasts of Fortune, when she is adverse, rush more dangerously at high persons than at the middle or the low. And on that subject, Boethius says in his second book that bad Fortune is of more profit than good Fortune, for good Fortune blinds with her benefits, and makes one believe in a secure state, and perverse Fortune reveals the reality of her mutability and the fact that one must not trust her.[7]

Here I speak of wicked and cruel men and how they are at the same time punished in this world.

On the subject mentioned above, that perils are great even for good and virtuous men, and that they are not totally exempted from them in spite of many good deeds, since God wills it at any time for their purgation in this world, or for the increase of their merits through patience, as Saint Augustine says, then indeed those wicked men should not be sure of themselves, but rather they should tremble and be afraid--those evil men, full of venom and false ambition, persecutors and destroyers of humankind, avid to shed blood and do any evil[8]--and in the Christian religion there are many such men nowadays, more than ever (which is a great pity), and, what is worse, they do not spare their likes, nor have any regard for their kinfolk, parents, and other relatives. Oh, blind and ignorant people, outside of God's law! Do those who act in such a way not know that life

[7]Boethius, *De consolatione philosophiae,* 2.8.
[8]Augustine, *De Civitate Dei,* 19.4.

si briefve et que au departir on n'en emporte ne mais le bien
ou le mal que on a fait, et que se pensent-ilz? Et s'il est
ainsi que Dieu nous dampne se nous n'amons et faisons bien
a noz prouchains selon Son saint commandement, que fera Il
donques de ceulx qui non pas seulement ne les aiment, mais   5
qui si vilainement les persecutent sans cause et occient?
Certes, je ne doubte pas que se grace Dieu--dont ilz ne sont
dignes--ne les en garde par leur donner advertissement de si
grans faultes, que la sentence divine ne chee sur eulx quelque fois si durement que dés en cestui monde, par punicion   10
juste, leur enfer ne commence.

   Comme de ce aïons mains exemples en la Sainte Escripture, si comme de Caym qui ot occis par traïson son frere
Abel; ne fu il aussi tuez par vengence de Dieu estrangement
a l'eure que le moins s'en gaitoit, tout se alast-il tapis-   15
sant par les bois, par Lameth, qui goute ne veoit, et aleoit
bersoiant la sauvagine, ne faire ne le cuidoit, si qu'il est
escript ou *Livre de genesis*? Aussi Absalon, qui son pere
persecutoit, ne fut-il par voulenté de Dieu qui plus ne le
pot souffrir, pendus diversement par les cheveux a un arbre   20
si comme il fuioit, et la miserablement d'un glaive occis,
si qu'il appert ou *Livre des roys*? Le roy Saul, qui par son
enuie persecutoit David, ne se occit-il lui meismes pour
plus estre villainement punis par dueil et rage de ce qu'a
venir ne povoit a sa faulse entencion?   25

   Et ainsi de pluseurs puis dire pour ramener a preuve
exemples plus auttentiques, prins en la Sainte Escripture,
que vray soit la fin d'iceulx mauvés estre miserable. Car
si que dit Theodolet, le sang des persecutez crie contre eulx
a leur souverain juge; si qu'il appert de Pharaon, le roy   30
d'Egipte, par le cui commandement et edit, tous les enfans
du peuple de Dieu estoient livrez a mort. Il fu enfin vitu-
perablement plungiez en la mer a toute sa puissance. O,
n'est pas mençongiere la parole de Dieu qui dit: "Contre
yceulx qui de glaive fiert, de glaive perist!" Car les   35
murtriers qui orent occis Hysboseth, David n'espargna pas la
griefve punicion. Item, Andronicus, qui pluseurs avoit fait
morir, ne fut-il aussi occis ou propre lieu ou avoit fait le
delit, si qu'il appert au *Second livre des Machabees*?
Gedeon ne prist-il la vengence comme vaillant de Zebee et   40
Salmana qui orent occis ses freres, si qu'il appert ou *Livre
des juges*? Achab, qui par sa convoitise fist mourir Naboth,
fu lourdement punis quant les chiens le mangierent et par

   28. mauvés *was in margin*

in this world is very brief, and when one leaves it, one does
not take along either the good or the evil that one has done;
and what do they think? For just as God condemns us if we
do not love or do not do good to our neighbors according to
His commandments, what will He do then to those who not only   5
do not love them but also persecute them so hideously without
a cause and kill them? Indeed, I do not doubt that if God's
grace--of which they are not worthy--does not protect them
by warning them of so many great faults, the divine sentence
will fall upon them at some time so severely that, while   10
still in this world their hell will start by a just punishment.

    For we have many examples of this in the Holy Scrip-
tures, such as Cain who treacherously killed his brother
Abel; was he not also strangely slain by the will of God at a   15
time when he was not in the least watchful, hiding in the
woods, by Lamech, who could not see at all and was hunting in
the wilds and did not think that he would do it, as it is
written in the *Book of Genesis*?[9] The same with Absalom, who
tormented his father, was he not, by the will of God, who   20
could not tolerate it any longer, hanged in a strange way by
the hair from a tree as he was fleeing, and killed miserably
by a sword, as it is said in the *Book of Kings*?[10] King
Saul, who persecuted David with torments, did he not kill
himself to stop being punished even more hideously by grief   25
and rage because he could not succeed in his wicked scheme?[1]

    And as proof, I can tell several more authentic exam-
ples taken from the Holy Scriptures to show that the end of
those wicked men is miserable. As Theodolus says,[2] the
blood of the martyrs cries against them to the sovereign   30
Judge, as is shown by Pharaoh, the King of Egypt, by whose
command and edict all the children of God's people were to be
put to death. In the end he was shamefully thrown in the sea
with all his power. Oh, the word of God does not lie when
it says: "Whoever kills by the sword, dies by the sword!"[3]   35
For the murderers who had killed Ishbosheth, David did not
spare a severe punishment.[4] Similarly, Andronicus, who had
had several people killed, was he not also killed in the
very spot where he had committed the crime, as is shown in
the *Second Book of Maccabees*?[5] Did the valiant Gideon not   40
take vengeance on Zebah and Zalmunna, who had slain his
brothers, as it is shown in the *Book of Judges*?[6] Ahab, who
had Naboth killed out of jealousy, was severely punished

[9]*Genesis* 4.16-24. [10]*2 Samuel* 18.9-15 (not the *Book of
Kings*). [1]*1 Samuel* 31.4. [2]Theodulus, *Ecloga.* [3]*Matthew*
26.52. [4]*2 Samuel* 4.12. [5]*2 Maccabees* 9.28. [6]*Judges* 8.21.

les champs le traynerent, si que dit le *Livre des roys*.
Athalie, la faulse royne, qui faisoit occire toute la lignee
royale, comment morut-elle miserablement? N'en ot pas moins
Bruneheut qui semblablement le faisoit? Jonas, le desloyal
tirant, qui ot fait occire Zacharie pour ce que preudoms   5
estoit, refu occis par ses propres serviteurs. Semblablement
Benadab le fu par le commandement de Dieu, si qu'il est
escript ou *Livre des roys*.

Et, a dire des vengences de Dieu, folz est qui ne les
doubte! Certes, ne puet estre plus vituperable mort que   10
occire soy meismes par desespoir, si que Dieu l'a permis a
de grans pecheurs, comme de Zambri, qui bien desservi la
mort, car quel plus grant mal puet estre commis que de mettre
la main a son souverain seigneur ou le persecuter? Car ainsi
cellui desloial l'ot fait a son roy, pour la quel cause,   15
quant vit que eviter ne povoit la vengence que sur soy ne
venist, il meismes, par desespoir bouta le feu ou palais ou
il estoit et ainsy peri, si que escript est ou *Livre des
roys*.

Et ainsi viennent estrangement et par diverses voies sur   20
les mauvais, quant garde ne s'en donnent, les vengences de
Dieu par divers cas; et mesmement, comme ce soit a condicion
de femme chose extraordinaire et contre sa nature de faire
occision, neantmoins pour plus deshonnourablement punir mains
chetifs, a Dieu voulu que par femmes aient esté occis, si   25
comme Abimeleth, qui a grant tort ot occis pluseurs freres,
mais d'une femme il fu occis. Semblablement le fu Sisara, le
trés mauvais tirant persecuteur, fina sa detestable vie par
la main d'une femme, si qu'il est escript ou *Livre des juges*.
Ainsi en avint-il au persecuteur du peuple de Dieu, Olo-   30
fernes, comme il appert au *Livre de Judith*. Et pour tant dit
l'Euvangille que quoy que necessité soit que aucune foiz esclandre viengne, neantmoins maudiçon est sur cellui par qui
esclandre, et dit en suivant que mieulx seroit pour tel homme
que on l'eust getté en la mer, une meule de molin au col.   35
Ha, comment ceste parole, qui ne puet mentir, fait bien
a noter a ceulx qui sont cause de maints maulx et tribulacions! Et qu'en dirioie? Toutes en sont plaines les Saintes
Escriptures et autres hystoires des vengences de Dieu sur les
effundeurs de sang a la parfin--quoyque Dieu a la foys   40

40. a la foys *was in margin*

14

when dogs devoured him and dragged him through the fields, as
the *Book of Kings* says.[7] Athaliah, the untrue queen who had
all the royal lineage slain, did she not die ignominiously?[8]
Did Brunhild receive less, who did the same?[9] Joash, the
immoral tyrant, who had Zachariah killed because he was a   5
wise man, was slain in turn by his own servants.[10] So was
Benhadad by God's command, as is written in the *Book of
Kings*.[1]

Yes, whoever doubts God's vengeance is a fool! Indeed,
there cannot be a more horrible death than to kill oneself   10
out of despair, just as God allowed it to some great sinners,
such as Zimri, who well deserved his death, for is there a
greater evil than to lay hands on one's sovereign lord and to
torment him? That is what this disloyal man did to his king,
and that is why, when he saw that he could not escape ven-   15
geance, out of despair, he set fire to the palace where he
was and so perished, as it is written in the *Book of Kings*.[2]

And so God's acts of vengeance come strangely and in
various ways upon the wicked when they are not careful; and
similarly, although it is an extraordinary thing for a woman   20
to kill because of her social condition and because it is
against her nature to kill, nevertheless, to punish many evil
men more dishonorably, God willed that some should be slain
by women, such as Abdimelech, who killed most wrongly several
brothers but was killed by a woman.[3] So was Sisera, the most   25
wicked tyrant and persecutor, who ended his detestable life
by a woman's hand, as is written in the *Book of Judges*.[4]
The same happened to the persecutor of God's people, Holo-
fernes, as is shown in the *Book of Judith*.[5] And on that
subject, the Gospel says that although scandalous deeds   30
sometimes occur, the one who makes it happen is nevertheless
damned, and it also says that it would be better for such a
man to have been cast into the sea, with a millstone around
his neck.[6]

Ah, how these words, which cannot lie, should be noticed 35
by those who are the cause of so many evils and tribulations!
And what shall I say about them? The Holy Scriptures and
other stories are all filled with God's final vengeance on
those who shed blood--although God at the same time suffers
and waits--such as Nero, Julian the Apostate, Denys the   40

[7]*1 Kings* 22.38. [8]*2 Chronicles* 23.21. [9]Brunhild, wife
of Sigebert, carried on a struggle against Fredegund, the
Frankish nobles, and her nephew Lothar who had her tortured
and executed. [10]*2 Chronicles* 24.20-22. [1]*1 Kings* 22.
[2]*1 Kings* 16.18. [3]*Judges* 9.53. [4]*Judges* 4.21-22. [5]*Judith*
13.6-9. [6]*Luke* 17.3 and *Matthew* 18.6-7.

longuement seuffre et attende--comme de Neron, Julien
l'Apostat, Denis le Tirant et infinis autres, mauvaisement
mors par leurs demerites. Et qui plus est, sces-tu quelz
reliques et fumee aprés d'eulx il demeure au monde, a non
Dieu? Diffame et despris et male renommee.   5

   *Cy commence a parler de .v. principaulx causes qui
mouvoir doivent a avoir pacience en mort d'amis. Et premierement de .ii. raisons et encores de la susditte prison.*

   Au premier propos retorner, ma trés redoubtee Dame, les
susdis exemples produis afin de principal cause te ramente- 10
voir d'avoir pacience et prendre reconfort en ta susditte
douleur de la mort de tes bons amis, pues veoir que plourer
ne les dois, mais a grant joye Dieu moult louer, pour .v.
principaulx raisons. La premiere est, veu que la Dieu grace
onques yceulx ne furent de cruauté blasmez et pour ce tu   15
pues penser que le droiturier juge, moïennant sa sainte
misericorde, a terminé les jours, non mie ainsi comme aux
mauvais diffamez dessusdis, mais a la fin des bons et des
bien renommez.
   La seconde cause touche la susdicte prison de ceste vie   20
humaine, dont par don de Dieu yceulx sont bien saillis, de
la quelle dicte prison, dit Saint Pol qu'il n'y a seurté en
nul des estas, ne en quelconques place, si que devant est ja
touchié et que experience le nous demoustre meismes des
mieulx fortunez et de ceulx que reputons les plus eureux.   25
Car qui est cil ou celle, quelque grant qu'il soit, qui
vanter se puist de passer sa vie ou sans diverses maladies,
ou sans grant travail de corps et occupacion de pensee, ou
sans aucune desplaisant subjection et soussy en quelque
guise ou il ait maintes amertumes et desplaisans ennuis?   30
Car dit Boece: "Je croy que onques nul fu en ce monde en si
grant prosperité que assez n'eust meslé avec de grans tribulacions, perilz, desplaisirs et maintes amertumes." Dont
dit Maximien: "O, vie humaine, tant es miserable comme
tousjours en peril de mort, sans seurté, n'aucune esta-   35
bleté!" Et de ceste chose, ma trés redoubtee Dame, toy en
personne, tout soies-tu trés haute princesse, es assez
aprise par pure experience en divers cas, je ne doubt mie,
et maintes aventures, comme Paradis ne soit a nul en ce
monde; et pour ce, les anciens sages desprisoient ceste vie, 40
dont, dit Lattance, que la mort est le desir des savans;
disoit Maximien: "O, vie humaine, tant est folz qui moult

Tyrant, and many others who all died ignominiously by their
own demerits. And what is more, do you know what relics and
smoke remain in the world after them, in the name of God?
Infamy, contempt, and ill repute.

Here I begin to talk about five principal causes which   5
must encourage patience at the death of friends. First, I
give two reasons; then more about the aforementioned prison.

To go back to my first subject, my Very Revered Lady, I
gave the aforementioned examples to remind you of the main
reason for having patience and taking comfort in your   10
aforesaid grief over the loss of your good friends, and that
you can see that you must not cry for them, but take great
joy in praising God, and that for five principal reasons.
The first is: since these men, by the grace of God, were
never accused of cruelty, that because of it you can imagine   15
that the fair Judge, with the help of His holy mercy, ended
their days, not in the same manner of the aforementioned
wicked and dishonorable men, but in the manner of good and
honorable men.

The second reason concerns the aforesaid prison of this   20
human life, which the latter have left in a good manner by
the grace of God, and of this said prison, Saint Paul says
that there is no security in any position or any location,
as I said before and as it is shown to us by experience,
even for the most fortunate men and for those whom we think   25
are the happiest.[7] For who is he or she, however powerful,
who can boast of having lived life without illness, or without great bodily fatigue or preoccupation of mind, or without any unpleasant problem or worry of any kind, or without
many a disappointment, or disagreeable trouble? On this   30
subject, Boethius says: "I believe that there never was
anyone whose grand prosperity was not mixed with great tribulations, dangers, displeasures, and many disappointments."[8]
Maximianus said on this subject: "Oh, human life, you are so
miserable, and you always fear of death, with neither secur-   35
ity nor stability!"[9] My Very Revered Lady, although you are
a high princess, you yourself know this by sheer experience
through various events and many happenings, I do not doubt,
since Paradise is of no one in this world: And this is the
reason why the ancient wise men despised this life for, as   40
Lactantius says, death is the wise man's wish;[10] and

[7]*Hebrews* 13.14. [8]Boethius, *De consolatione philosophiae,*
2. [9]Maximianus, *Elegia.* [10]Lactantius, *De ira Dei*(?).

te prise, comme tu soies trés miserable et as .iii. especiales condicions moult reprochables, c'est assavoir: tu es trés briefve; secondement, en toy n'a point de repos; tiercement souffisance n'y a!" Et pour ce dit Macrobe que la vraie philosophie est d'avoir devant les yeulx la briefté de ceste   5 vie, car penser a la mort, dit-il, fait l'omme sage et soy meismes congnoistre. Et dit Seneque que le sage homme doit a toute heure avoir a memoire le trespas de la mort tout ainsy comme le pelerin a au devant des yeulx, ne oublier ne le puet, le perilleux trespas par ou passer lui convient   10 ains que chés lui retorne. Et pour tant, trés noble Dame, ces dittes choses considerees et assez d'autres que je laisse pour briefté, dois estre appaisiee et assez contente dont yceulx que tu amoies sont saillis de ceste susdicte miserable prison.   15

Cy dit de la tierce raison qui doit mouvoir a reconfort selon Seneque et autres autteurs.

La tierce raison, qui mouvoir te doit, est ce que meismes recite Seneque en son *Livre des remedes de Fortune* ou il dit: "Tu qui ploures tes amis mors, de quoy te plains,   20 ne quel tort reçois-tu? Car n'ont-il receu chose qui commune ne soit a tous? Dont ne savoies-tu que mortelz estoient et que en ce monde de par tel condicion entrerent que yssir en devoient?" Et de ce dit Job: "Homme est de brieve vie, plaine de misere et de povreté, legierement aneantist comme   25 la fleur et, comme l'ombre, de lieu en lieu s'enfuit; ainsi trespasse la vie de l'omme en briefveté et legierement." Et dit Seneque: "Le pelerinage de ceste vie n'est-il tel, que aprés que on aura moult alé, que l'en retorne arriere ou lieu dont on est venu? Pour ce nul glorifier d'aage ne se   30 doit, comme du passé il ne soit plus riens, de cil a venir n'y a seurté combien il durera. Est-ce donques chose nouvelle," dit Seneque, "que morir? Ne vient mort en toutes maisons, a la quelle dés que nous naissons nous y met nature terme?" Pour ce dit Maximien: "Le temps tire aprés lui   35 toutes choses morteles, et ainsy comme le ciel tourne, semblablement une vie court aprés lui."

A propos d'amis mors, dit oultre Seneque: "A quoy ploures ce que tien n'estoit? Fortune prestez les t'avoit,

38. Seneque *crossed out, followed by* oultre Seneque

18

The Prison of Human Life

Maximianus says: "Oh, human life, whoever values you is a
fool, because you are miserable and have three very shameful
attributes, that is: you are very brief; secondly, there is
no tranquility in you; thirdly, there is no satisfaction in
you!"[1] On this subject, Macrobius says that the true philos-   5
ophy is to keep in mind the brevity of life, since to think
of death makes a man wise and know himself.[2] And Seneca
says that the wise man must remember death at all times, just
as the pilgrim keeps it in front of his eyes and cannot forget the dangerous passage through which he has to go before   10
he can go home.[3] My Very Noble Lady, after considering these
things that I have said, and others that I omit for brevity's
sake, you should be comforted and even happy for those whom
you love, since they have left this aforementioned miserable
prison.   15

*Here I will speak of the third reason which should give
comfort according to Seneca and other authors.*

The third reason which should move you is what Seneca
himself writes in his *Book on the Remedies against Fortune*,
where he says: "You who cry over your deceased friends,   20
what is your complaint, what wrong is done to you? Did they
not receive something that is common to all of us? Did you
not know that they were mortal, and that after they had
entered this world in such condition they had to leave it?"
Job says on this subject: "Man's life is short, full of   25
miseries and of poverty; it is softly annihilated like a
flower, and like a shadow it flees from place to place; thus
ends man's life briefly and swiftly."[4] Seneca says: "Is
the pilgrimage of this life not such that, after one has
gone far, one must go back to where one came from? For this   30
reason no one must glorify time, since time past is no more
and it is uncertain how long the time to come will last.[5]
Is dying something new?" Seneca asks, "Does death not come
to all houses, and does nature not put a term to our own
death as soon as we are born?"[6] Maximianus says: "Time   35
draws all mortal things, and just as the sky turns, so a
life runs after it."[7]
On the subject of dead friends, Seneca adds: "Why do
you cry after what was not yours? Fortune had lent them to

[1]Maximianus, *Elegia*. [2]In Macrobius' commentary of
Cicero's *Somnium Scipionis* 1.9. [3]Pseudo-Seneca, *De remediis
fortuitorum.* [4]*Job* 14.1-2. [5]Pseudo-Seneca, *De remediis
fortuitorum.* [6]*Ibid.* [7]Maximianus, *Elegia*.

se elle les t'a retolus, de quoy te plains?" Et dit Ovide
que l'aage d'omme est comme l'eaue qui tousjours court et
jamais ne retourne. Pour ce disoit Seneque: "O, comme fole
chose est doubter ce que ne puet estre eschevé! Car quoyque
on retarde, si convient-il en fin par mort passer. Donques,   5
tu, qui muers,"dist-il,"es-tu le premier ou le derrain?
N'est-ce l'office de l'umaine espece?" A ce propos, le
philosophe Secondus dit a soy-mesmes: "O, qu'est-ce que
homme?" Et puis respont et dit: "Certes, c'est une fantasme
qui tantost trespasse, ne il n'est autre chose ne mais le   10
vaissel de mort, le pelerin sans repos, l'oste de la terre et
viande de vers." "Pourquoy," dit Seneque, "doit la chose
estre griefve qui a tous est commune? Ne scet-on que toutes
choses crees ça jus ont commencement et fin? Et donques,
qui paie la debte n'en est-il quitte? Et se tu plains tes   15
amis, dist-il, pour ce que mors sont en bataille, c'est grant
folie, car pour tant ne leur fu la mort plus dure qu'en autre
part, la quelle ou que ce soit, ne puet estre receue ne mais
une foiz, ne li homs frappez de pluseurs plaies, morir ne
puet forz d'une mort."   20
    Et a propos de ce dit Aristote, et a ce s'accordent tous
sages et meismement Caton en son livre, que mort qui a tous
est naturel passage, ne doit estre redoubtee pour bien faire,
c'est assavoir aux chevaliers pour la deffence de leur prince
et la chose publique, ne les sages a dire verité pour peril   25
de mort. Et pour tant les Anciens louerent moult les chevalereux qui, pour soustenir droiture, exposoient leurs
corps; de quoy, dit Seneque, que quoyque pou de chose soit
vie d'omme, neantmoins est trés grant vertu et trés louable
a cellui qui pou la prise; car adont est-il hardis et seur   30
en toutes places, soit en mer, en terre, en bataille ou autre
part. Et raconte Xenophon, que le roy Cirus, qui tant fu en
son temps chevalereux, tenoit si petit compte de sa vie,
qu'en tous perilz trés hardiement s'abondonnoit, pour quoy,
quant vint a mort, disoit a ceulx qui presents estoient: 35
"Mes amis et enfans, j'ay tousjours eu si a memoire la vie
seconde, que quant je seray mort, ne cuidiez que je aille en
païs nouvel, car je ne iray fors ou païs ou mon cuer a tousjours esté." Si dit a propos Seneque: "Se tu muers hors de
ton païs, et que t'en chault quant de toutes terres a che-   40
mins, pour aler en l'autre monde qui est ton droit païs? Et
se jeune tu muers, de ce, que pers-tu, puisque une fois le

you, and if she takes them back, what is your complaint?"[8]
Ovid says that man's time is like the water, which flows and
never returns. Seneca says about that: "Oh, what a foolish
thing it is to fear what cannot be avoided! For however one
puts it off, one has to go through death in the end. There-   5
fore, you who are dying, are you the first or the last? Is
it not the duty of the human species?"[9] On this subject,
the philosopher Secondus tells himself: "Oh, what is man?"
He answers thus: "Indeed, he is an illusion which soon
disappears; he is nothing but the vessel of death, the rest-   10
less pilgrim, the guest of the earth and the food of worms."
"Why," Seneca says, "must this thing, common to all, be
painful? Do we not know that all things created down here
have a beginning and an end? Therefore, whoever pays the
debt, is he not free of it? And it is great folly to pity   15
your friends," he says, "because they died in battle, since
their deaths were not worse than in any other place, since
death, wherever it occurs, can be received only once, just
as the man stricken by many wounds can only die once."[10]
Aristotle says on this subject--and all the wise men   20
agree with him, including even Cato in his book[1]--that death
which is a natural passage for all, must not be feared when
one does good: that is, by the knights when they defend
their prince and the government, or by the wise men when
they tell the truth under the threat of death.[2] This is why   25
the Ancients highly praised the knightly men who offered
their bodies to uphold justice, and Seneca said that although man's life has little value, nevertheless, whoever
does not value it much has great virtue and deserves praise;
thus he is bold and secure everywhere, be it at sea, on   30
land, in battle, or anywhere else.[3] Xenophon tells us that
King Cyrus, who was very knightly in his time, valued his
life so little that he rushed very boldly into any danger,
and this is why, when he was dying, he said to all present:
"My friends and children, I have always borne in mind the   35
life to come to such a degree that when I die, do not think
that I will go to a new land, for I will go to no land
except where my heart has always been."[4] Seneca says about
that: "If you die outside of your country, what does it
matter how many roads in all lands there are which go to the   40
other world, which is your rightful land? And if you die
young, what do you lose by it, since you must die sometime?

[8]Pseudo-Seneca, *De remediis fortuitorum.* [9]*Ibid.*
[10]*Ibid.* [1]In *Disticha Catonis.* [2]Aristotle, probably from
Ethica Nichomachea, 3.8. [3]Pseudo-Seneca, *De remediis
fortuitorum.* [4]Xenophon, *Cyropedia*, 8.7.

te convient? Et par celle fin, tu eschieves les dangiers de
viellece qui ne sont pas petis et les infortunes et males
aventures qui en longue vie a venir te pourroient. Si est
ton meilleur," dist-il,"morir, quant a vivre te delittes que
tant attendre qu'ennuiez en feusses." 5

Cy dit de pacience et de quoy elle sert.

Oultre ces choses, ains que je tire a conclusion cest
present dittié, me trés redoubtee Dame, je, ton humble servante obeissant, qui a tous tes maulx, ennuis, et desplaisirs vouldroie--et ce scet Dieu se en puissance m'estoit-- 10
toute m'emploier a y remedier, avisant et considerant que
non pas seulement a la susditte cause de mort d'amis--
combien que moult grief te soit et ait esté--soient tes
tribulacions, mais aussi pour achoison d'autres choses si
comme chascun scet dures a porter a ton loyal et amant 15
courage--Dieux par sa grace, selon ton bon desir, t'en
vueille getter hors, et semblablement soit a maintes nobles
dames et damoiselles; comme les tribulacions de ce monde en
maintes choses soient a passer tant dures, souvent avient et
a pluseurs personnes que a pou plus doulce est mort, est bon 20
d'aviser se aucunement pourroit estre trouvee medicine par
quelque voye pour le mal de tribulacion mitiguer et assou-
agier, dont, sans issir du propos cy devant promis de toy
assigner et rendre assez raisons de reconfort, ay, ma Dame,
pour l'amour de toy, tant cerchié es Sains Livres que 25
trouvee ay la benoite huile que les douleurs d'aversité puet
garir et saner, de la quelle, aprés les medecins de noz ames
qui la nous ont escripte, te diray la recepte et ses pro-
prietez; ceste s'appelle en .ii. manieres qui toutes revien-
nent a une. L'un s'appelle: espoire en Dieu et fay bien, 30
par cestui nom l'appella David le prophete; l'autre nom est
dit: souffrir paciemment pour l'amor de Nostre Seigneur.
Du premier nom d'esperance, comme ce soit chose a
l'avoir sur toutes necessaire contre le mors de tribulacion
pensant que tousjours ne durera ce que ainsi--se Dieu plaist 35
a toy aviengne--dist Nostre Seigneur: "Ceulx qui espereront
en moy ne decherront de leur desir", et dit le Psalmiste:
"Beneuré est cellui qui a fiance en Nostre Seigneur, car
c'est le seul refuge de tribulacion." Et veult dire oultre--
comme Nostre Seigneur soit tout bon et tout poissant et ne 40
desprise le cuer humilié du vray repentant et depriant--soit
toute nostre fiance en lui, car sa misericorde qui ne puet

By doing so, you avoid the dangers of old age, which are
great, and the misfortunes and bad things that could happen
to you in a long life. Therefore, it is better for you,"
he says, "to die while you enjoy living than to wait so long
that you become worried by it." [5]   5

Here I speak of patience and its usefulness.

    In addition to these things, before I draw this present
treatise to a conclusion, my Very Revered Lady, I, your humble and obedient servant, would like to find a remedy for
all your troubles, worries, and misfortunes--and God knows   10
if this is in my power--knowing and considering that your
tribulations are due not only to the aforementioned cause of
the deaths of friends--although this is and has been very
painful to you--but also to other things that are, as anyone
knows, hard to bear in your loyal and loving heart--would   15
that God by His grace might get you out of them as you would
wish. He would act similarly towards many noble ladies and
young girls, because the tribulations of this world in many
ways are so difficult to bear--often it is the case, and for
not a few persons, that death is easier [to bear]--it is   20
good to consider if any cure could be found to lessen and
soften the pain of these tribulations; this is why, without
leaving the previous purpose promised to offer you and give
you many reasons to find comfort, I have, my Lady, out of
love of you, searched so much in the Holy Books that I have   25
found the Holy Unction which can cure and heal the pains of
adversity, according to the doctors who wrote about it for
our souls, and I will give you the prescription and its
properties: There are two and both are one. One is called:
hope in God and doing good, as David the Prophet called it;[6]   30
the other name is: suffering patiently for the love of Our
Lord.
    Concerning the first name, hope, since it is something
necessary to have above all others against the pain of
suffering in order to think that this pain will not last   35
forever--if it please God that such should happen--Our Lord
says: "Those who have faith in me will not be disappointed
in their desire";[7] and the Psalmist says: "Blessed is he
who trusts Our Lord, because He is the only refuge from
tribulation."[8] This also means: because Our Lord is all   40
good and all powerful and does not reject the humble heart
of the truly repentant and praying man, that our trust in

[5]Pseudo-Seneca, *De remediis fortuitorum.* [6]*Psalms* 31.7.
[7]*Ibid*, 90.9. [8]*Ibid*, 83.13.

faillir, durera par tous siecles. De cette fiance en Dieu
et parfaite esperance, le priant de bon cuer, sont toutes
plaines les Saintes Escriptures, la quelle pour ton secours,
noble Dame, vueilles tousjours en toutes tribulacions
prendre pour ta part comme bon remede et trés secourable.   5

De l'autre, qui est de souffrir et qui bien te touche,
veult ainsi dire Saint Basile: "Pour ce que tribulacions
sont communes en tous les estas, Nostre Sire a voulu que par
ycelles, moyennant pacience, de toutes gens puissent aler
ou ciel, comme il soit impossible de passer de delices en   10
delices, c'est assavoir avoir tous ses plaisirs et aises en
cestui mortel monde et aler par ycelles en la joye du ciel,
qui ne puet estre." De ceste pacience, comme Nostre
Seigneur nous en donnast en sa propre personne exemple, qui
plus souffri que onques ne fist autre mortel homme, pouvons, 15
par l'en suivre, esperer celle voye estre sur toutes salu-
taire, si dit Basille: "O, tu homme qui desires vaincre
toutes choses et obtenir vittoire, se tu veulz a ce a venir,
prens pacience pour escu et va hardiement en la bataille des
tribulacions et, se bien t'en deffens, riens ne te surmon-   20
tera, ains en istras vainqueur et vittorieux." O, de ceste
medicine de pacience, comment en ont parlé tous les sains
dotteurs, et que est-elle recommandee en la Sainte Escripture!

Et pour tant, redoubtee Dame, que elle t'est neccess-   25
saire, t'en vueil encore un petit parler. De ceste vertu
avoir, dit de rechief Saint Basille: "Qui avec soy heberge
pacience, il hostele Jhesu Crist." Aussi dit l'Euvangille:
"Beneurez sont les paciens, car filz de Dieu seront
appellez"; dit oultre: "Et se les martirs sont hault   30
eslevez es cieulx pour leur merite par dessus les autres
ordres des sains, pourquoy aussi ne le seroient ceulx qui
tourmentez sont par diverses tribulacions et paciemment les
portent pour l'amour de Nostre Seigneur? Donques, entre
vous mondains," dist-il, "pourquoy vous laissiez-vous vain-   35
cre a impacience quant votre arbitre et retribueur des
merites a appareillié la couronne pour les bien souffrans?"
Et dit Saint Pristien: "O, homme, que tu es folz, quant par
ton impacience qui riens ne te puet proufiter, ains assez
nuire, tu pers l'eritage qui t'est promis! Car Dieu a   40
commandé les paciens et paisibles avoir possession en sa
maison, afin que ilz habitent en paix avec leur pere Jhesu
Crist, au quel bien ne pevent a venir, fors par vaincre les
tribulacions en souffrant."

Him must be complete, since His mercy, which cannot fail, will endure throughout the centuries. Of this faith and perfect hope in God, if we pray to Him sincerely, the Holy Scriptures are full; may you, for your relief, Noble Lady, use them yourself forever in all tribulations as a good and very helpful remedy. 5

Of the other name, which is suffering, and indeed applies to you, Saint Basil says this: "Because tribulations are common to all classes, Our Lord has willed that through them, and by the means of patience, all people go to Heaven, 10 since it is impossible to go from delight to delight, that is, to have all pleasures and comforts in this mortal world and go through them to the joy of Heaven, which is a thing that cannot be." From this patience, as Our Lord gave us as an example in His very person, He who suffered more than any 15 mortal man ever has, we can, following Him in this, hope to find His path a salvation above all others; so Saint Basil says: "Oh, man, you who wish to vanquish all things and obtain victory, if you wish to succeed in this, have patience as your shield and go bravely to the battle of tribulations, 20 and if you defend yourself well against them, nothing will defeat you, and you will come out of it a conqueror and a victor." Oh, how much all the holy doctors have written about the medicine of patience, and how highly it is recommended in the Holy Scriptures! 25

Therefore, Revered Lady, I want to say a little more about why it is a necessity for you. Saint Basil says again on possessing this virtue: "Whoever lodges patience, houses Jesus Christ."[9] The Gospel also says: "Blessed be the patient, for they will be called God's sons", and it also 30 says: "and if the martyrs are placed high in the Heavens above the other orders of saints, why would those not be placed there also who are tormented by tribulations and suffer them patiently for the love of Our Lord? Therefore," it says, "you men on earth, why are you overcome by impa- 35 tience when your judge and distributor of merits has prepared a crown for those who have suffered well?"[10] Saint Priscian says: "Oh, man, how foolish you are when because of your impatience which can profit you in no way and even harm you, you lose the inheritance which was promised to you! 40 Because God has ordered that the patient and the peaceful should have possession of His house to live in peace with their Father Jesus Christ, and they can come to this happiness only by defeating the tribulations that they suffer."[1]

[9]These quotations may come from Basil's *Epistolae*.
[10]*Matthew* 5.10-12. [1]Priscian, *Institutiones grammaticae*.

*Cy dit encores de pacience et comment elle doit estre
entendue en ce qui touche Justice.*

De ces tribulacions porter paciemment, avant que plus
passe oultre, afin de mieulx entendre et a parler clerement
pour ce que aucunes questions pourroient estre faites, a   5
savoir se pour obeir a pacience on est tenu d'endurer les
torffais receus du prouchain et caetera..., pour venir a
respondre a ceste question, est a savoir que par .ii. manieres d'occasions viennent et sourdent communement trouble-
mens de courage et contaminacions de pensee; dont l'une   10
vient et est la pire, et qui plus a haute gent messiet a
cause d'orgueil et oultrecuidance ou de mauvaise acoustu-
mance par la mignotise de trop aise de non vouloir riens
souffrir; la seconde est plus naturelle et assez excusable
selon les complexions ou les cas si que aprés sera dit.   15
La premiere que j'ay dit, qui d'orgueil vient, est
quant cuer d'omme est tant eslevé en arrogance, qu'il lui
semble qu'autre quelconque creature ne le vaille, et adont
est comme forsenez, quant tant soit petit est poingt d'aucun
pou de parole qui ne lui plaise ou que moins que neant lui   20
soit fait aucune chose oultre son gré, ou que il ait quelque
pou de perte; adont a son impacience n'y a resne tenue, mais
toute fureur qui n'est excusable en nulle maniere, ains trés
mortele, dampnable, et reprehensible. Dont de tel
orgueilleux, dit Josephus, que il decherra d'onneur et ne   25
vendra a fin de sa voulenté. Et Florus en dit, pour ce que
les folz arrogans n'ont regart a l'avantage de pacience qui
le cuer et les mouvemens du corps assouagist, de tant se
demoustre il moins sage, comme moins de pacience y est
apperceue, car la ou elle n'est, toutes vertus sont nulles.   30
"Le cuer arrogant," dist-il, "est tousjours tourmenté et en
tribulacion pour le dueil que a que tout le monde ne surmonte. Tel creature," dist-il, "est congneue a la face,
comme il l'ait tousjours furieuse, et par tous les signes
du corps demoustre son impacience et fureur de courage,   35
c'est assavoir le langage plain de menaces et felonnes
paroles."
Comme dit Saint Jehan: "La trés mauvaise langue de
l'orgueilleux est effusion de sang, les yeulx orribles en
regars, traversez et espoantables, la chiere pale, le front   40
suant, les mains debatans et tout le corps tremblant."

More about patience and how it must be understood when it concerns Justice.

On the subject of bearing these tribulations with patience, before I go on to something else, in order to understand them better and to make myself clear since questions could be asked, such as if to have patience one is bound to endure wrongdoings caused by someone, etc...., in order to arrive at an answer to this question, one should know that in two different ways lack of courage and bad thoughts come and appear frequently; one way, which is worse and ill befits the best people because of pride, vanity, and bad habit from too much delight and the unwillingness to suffer anything; the second way is more natural and can be excused depending on the circumstances or the cases that will be presented hereafter.

The first way that I mentioned, and which comes from pride, happens when a man's heart is so inflated in arrogance that it seems to him that no one can match his worth, and therefore he acts like a madman whenever the very unimportant words of someone are unpleasant to him, or an action worth less than nothing is done to him against his will, or when he has the smallest loss; then, he cannot put a stop to his impatience, but is in a furor which is never excusable in any way; rather, it is lethal, damnable and reprehensible. Josephus says about such a proud man that he will lose his honor, and his desire will come to naught. Florus says that, since foolish and arrogant men do not see that the benefit of patience is that it softens the heart and the movements of the body, they show themselves less wise because less patience can be seen, for wherever it is not present, all virtues are as naught. "The arrogant heart," he says, "is always tormented and in tribulation because of the unhappiness that he feels when he cannot dominate everyone. Such a creature," he says, "can be recognized because he shows a constantly furious face; and in all the movements of his body he shows his impatience and his angry heart also, because his language is full of threats and wicked words."[2]

As Saint John says: "The very evil language of the proud involves the flushing of blood, eyes casting horrible glances, looking fixed and fearsome, skin becoming pale, a brow sweating, hands moving about, and a shaking body."

[2]Probably in Florus' *Epitome bellorum omnium annorum DCC*, a very popular work in the medieval west.

La Prison de Vie Humaine

Dont d'un tel, dit ung sage: "O, homme, se tu te veoies
quant yre te surmonte furieusement, grant orreur auroies de
toy meismes en voiant tant orriblement ta face si comme
difformee et tout ton corps transmué." A propos de gens
ainsi passionez, dit Ysidore que ceulx, qui toute leur   5
felicité ont mise es choses du monde n'a autre riens n'ont
regart, ne porroit estre que souvent ne s'airassent, ne
estre en eulx pacience, la quelle est don de Dieu, du quel
avoir ne sont dignes. A ce s'accorde Josephus, en disant
que l'impacient qui par longue accoustumance de ne vouloir   10
riens souffrir tourmente autrui, mais en tourmentant les
autres, il tourmente lui-meismes et par ce commence son
enfer dés en cestui monde, le quel, aprés et a tousjours,
il possedera. Et de cestui sont nulles les tribulacions,
fors en tant que lui-meismes les se fait, si n'y a nulle   15
pitié.
       La seconde cause que je dis cy dessus dont tribulacion
de courage vient, qui plus est piteuse, naturele, et non si
reprehensible, est quant infortunes viennent a la personne
par aucunes voies, si comme de mort d'amis, de pertes de   20
biens, de dommages eus, injures et vilennies par autrui receues, temptacions d'ennemi, et de choses semblables en
divers cas; dont le courage se trouble, le quel troublement,
quant est de soy n'est une pechié, comme il ne soit en
puissance d'omme de non sentir les douleurs quant elles   25
viennent, mais voirs est que par trop y habonder sans
restrinction d'aucune pacience, on y puet errer et pechier.
Et cestes sont celles dont les Saintes Escriptures entendent,
dont la pacience est meritoire tant que est greigneur es
dures adversitez. Et avec ce, est a savoir que Nostre   30
Seigneur veult, si que tesmoingne son saint Euvangille, que
meismement on aime son ennemy et que pour lui on prie, et
que on soit plus dolent de ce que il grieve l'ame de lui-
meismes en persecutant et courrouce Dieu, que de l'injure
que on reçoit a l'exemple de Jhesu Crist, a qui plus desplut   35
le desespoir de Judas que de ce qu'il le ot trahy.
       Mais a revenir au propos de la question touchiee dessus:
se on est tenus de souffrir toutes injures, et caetera...,
est a savoir que ceste pacience avoir et amer son ennemy
n'est mie pour tant a entendre que Dieux, qui est droit juge, 40
ne vueille bien que cellui qui a tort est assaillis, [ne] se
deffende en droit et raison, soit en guerre a qui il appart-
tient, par plait ou autrement par voye de droit, et que par
deffense convenable garde sa chose; et se accusez est, que
il s'excuse et clarifie au monde sa juste cause ou le droit   45

The Prison of Human Life

A sage says of such a person: "Oh, man, if you could see
yourself when anger overcomes you, you would feel a deep
horror of yourself seeing your awful face so distorted and
your body so completely changed." On the subject of men thus
consumed by passion, Isidore says that those who have placed   5
their happiness in the affairs of this world and disregard
all other things cannot avoid being angry often; nor can they
have patience, which is a gift of God, and of which they are
not worthy.[3] Josephus agrees and says that the impatient one
who torments others because he has a long habit of not want-   10
ing to suffer anything, in tormenting others torments
himself, and so begins in this world the Hell which he will
have later and forever. And he does not go through tribulations, except those that he causes himself and for which
there is no respite.   15

The second reason mentioned above which comes from tribulation of the heart, and which is more pitiful, natural, and
less reprehensible, occurs when unfortunate things happen to
someone in different ways, such as when friends die, when one
loses his riches, suffers losses, receives insults and out-   20
rage from others, is tempted by the enemies, and from similar
things happening in various ways; the heart becomes troubled,
and though this is not a sin in itself, since man is not able
to avoid pains when they come, it is true that when they are
too frequent, without the help of patience one can err and   25
sin. These pains are those mentioned in the Holy Scriptures,
and patience is of greater value if the misfortunes are
deeper and more severe. And on that very subject, we have
to know what Our Lord wants, since it is said in His Holy
Gospel that, just as we must love our enemy and pray for him,   30
we must feel sorry for him because he pains his own soul in
causing suffering and angers God, more than he pains us,
following the example of Jesus Christ who grieved more from
Judas' despair than from the fact that he had betrayed Him.

But to come back to the question mentioned above: if   35
one must bear all insults, etc...., we have to know that to
have this patience and to love our enemy does not mean that
God, who is a fair judge, does not want that one who is
wrongly assaulted not to defend himself in all right and
reason, whether in war which is fitting for him, or in a   40
lawsuit, or in any other lawful means, or not to keep his
property with an appropriate defense; and if he is accused,
let him apologize and explain to everyone his case or the
case of his people, just as Ecclesiastes says: "Be mindful
of your good name."[4] Saint Basil says on that subject that   45

[3]Isidore, *Synonyma*.   [4]*Ecclesiastes* 7.2.

29

des siens; car meismes dit l'Ecclesiaste: "Aies cure de
bonne renommee." De ce dit Saint Basille que, qui de pacience fait targe, toutes durtez lui semblent legieres. Et
s'il est injurié par aucun, sa deffense est faite, non mie
par ire, vengence, ne impacience, mais pour garder le droit   5
a justice; car dit Jhesu Sirach: "Combas-toy pour justice,
et Dieux vaincra pour toy, mais pour pou de chose ne te trouble doleur, dont faire lui convient et en mettant paine de
pacifier son adversaire." Ceste patience, donques, n'est
autre chose ne mais attrempance de courage qui sousmet la   10
voulenté a tout ce qui plaist a Nostre Seigneur et pour
s'amour, vouloir endurer toutes choses paisiblement.
    Et pour ce que on dit, et il est vray, que pacience n'a
mie qui veult et ne se prent pas en la bourse; dit Ysidore
que c'est un tresor qui moult doit estre par grant diligence   15
acquis comme il soit trés valable meismement au corps et plus
a l'ame: au corps, en tant qu'il lui donne le don de paix et
seurté en ce qu'il ne doubte nulle male aventure, car il est
prest de tout porter et pour tant vit liement et en santé, ne
de riens ne souffie car il est seur en toutes places, ne For-   20
tune ne lui puet nuire. "Et toute somme," dist-il, "c'est la
fontaine des vertus, donnant trés nourissant et trés souef
boire a l'ame, car il la met hault emprés Jhesu Crist." La
maniere de la acquerir, dit qu'il convient, a qui la veult
avoir, regarder hault et non mie a terre, car elle vient du   25
ciel; c'est a savoir penser aux guerredons de la vie a venir
et ainsi passera legierement tous les maulx de ceste, tout
ainsi comme le chevalier qui se combat en la bataille oublie
toutes ses bleceures pour l'attente de la victoire. "O,"
dist-il aprés, "homme, pourquoy te doit estre ceste chose   30
griefve a faire, quant la vie de cest monde si tost passe
et celle a venir dure a tousjours? Se tu es marchant ou
d'autre estat ne souffriras-tu froit, chault, et maints
labours pour acquerre chevance? Donques, se tu seuffres
pour Paradis avoir, te dois-tu plaindre? Et se tu me dis   35
que tu es persecutez par les mauvais a tort et sans cause,
qui trop est chose a souffrir dure, je dis que tu es folz
en tant que tu t'en troubles, car mal ne te pevent faire
nulz ennemis se tu-meismes ne veulz; ains grandement
prouffite par bien endurer et si en es plus sage, dont vous   40
dit de rechief entre vous qui passez par le pelerinage de
ceste vie: aiez pacience et vous serez les chevaliers de
Jhesu Crist; bataillez fort contre les adversitez, et plus
promps soiez a recevoir maulx qu'a les faire; brisiez les
saïettes de contumelie et d'injure par souffrir, et mettez   45

whoever protects himself with patience will find all adversities light to bear. And if he is insulted by someone,
his defense will be accomplished not by anger, vengeance, nor
by impatience, but by guarding right with justice, as Jesus
Sirach says: "Fight for justice and God will win for you,   5
but do not let a little pain that He gives you trouble you
when He must trouble Himself to pacify His enemy.[5] Therefore, this patience is none other than moderation of heart
which submits the will to everything which pleases Our Lord,
and the will to endure all things peacefully for His love.   10

And it is said (and it is true) that not everyone who
wants it has patience, it is not a thing that comes from
one's purse: Isidore says that it is a treasure which must
be acquired through hard work since it is a great value to
the body and even more to the soul: to the body, inasmuch   15
as it gives it the gift of peace and security, and therefore it will not fear a bad experience for it is ready to
bear anything and thus lives happily and in good health; it
does not suffer from anything since it is safe in all places,
and Fortune cannot harm it. "To sum it all," he says, "it   20
is the fountain of virtues, which gives a very nourishing
and delightful drink to the soul, for it places it near
Jesus Christ." He says that the way to acquire patience for
whoever wants it is to look on high, and not down to earth,
since it comes from Heaven; in other words, we must think of   25
the rewards of the life to come, and in this way all the
evils of this life will pass swiftly, just as the knight who
in battle forgets his wounds in the hope of victory. "Oh,"
he says later, "man, why should this thing be hard for you
to do, when the life of this world goes by so quickly and   30
the one to come lasts forever? If you are a merchant or
from another estate, will you not suffer cold, heat, and
many travails to gain profits? Therefore, if you suffer to
gain Paradise, should you complain? And if you tell me that
you are persecuted by the wicked wrongly and without reason,   35
which is a very hard thing to bear, I say that you are a
fool if you pay attention to it, because no enemy can harm
you if you yourself do not want it; instead it is of great
benefit to suffer well and be wiser by it, and I will say
again to you, who are going through the pilgrimage of this   40
life: have patience and you will be the knights of Jesus
Christ; fight hard against adversities, and be readier to
receive evils than to do them; break the arrows of outrage
and insult by suffering and place first the study of
patience; do not seek vengeance for the wounds of words,   45

[5]*Ecclesiasticus* 4.3.

au devant l'estude pacience; ne vous contrevengiez de frap-
peures de langue, car c'est grant vertu de ne blecier cellui
qui a blecié et grant force de courage de non rendre mal pour
mal, les quelles choses commande Nostre Seigneur en Son Saint
Euvangille!" 5

*Cy dit de la .iiiie raison de reconfort de mort d'amis,
qui touche des amis qui sont demourez en vie et de .iii. dons
principaulx.*

Or revendray a nostre premiere matiere des causes de reconfort. La .iiiie. raison qui conforter te doit, redoubtee 10
Dame, est plus joïeuse quant au regart de la sensualité et
fragilité humaine, qui trop a paine se puet passer des
plaisirs de terre, les quelz, a voir dire, ne sont mie tous
vicieux, ains licites et honnestes, de telz y a, ne a Dieu ne
desplaisent. Et est l'argument que Boece en son *Livre de* 15
consolacion met, que Philosophie, entre les autres raisons de
reconfort, lui proposa et mist au devant quant lui rameuteut
les enfans qu'il avoit; c'est assavoir que comme il n'ait
esté, ne soit quelconque creature tant delaissiee de toute
bonne fortune que demouré ne lui soit aucun residu de cause 20
de reconfort--a la quel chose, trés noble Dame, la Dieu
grace, tu n'as pas failli, ains, Dieux mercis, en a largement
en pluseurs manieres et meismement plus que communement
autres dames n'ont--les quelles choses non recongnoistre,
seroit ingratitude, qui est grant pechié. Et pour tant, soit 25
averti ton bon courage et aies a memoire, en merciant Dieu
et meismement pour ton reconfort contre les assaulx et poin-
tures de tribulacion quant elles t'oppressent, les trés grans
et nobles benefices que as receus de ton Createur, qui t'en
doint bien user, les quelz sont .iii. en especiauté dont plu- 30
seurs autres biens viennent et dependent; c'est assavoir: le
don de grace, cellui de nature, et le don de fortune.
De ces .iii. dons afin de mieulx entendre est a savoir
que les .ii., quant nous les avons, sont dedens nous, et le
tiers est dehors. Cellui qui est dit de grace est en l'ame 35
de creature humaine, et cestui est l'entendement qui donne,
si comme dit Aristote, ymaginer et comprendre les choses qui
sont ou pevent estre, et congnoissance d'entendre et conce-
voir celles que on a veues, oÿés, et congnueues, et discer-
ner les unes des autres en eslisant les unes pour bonnes et 40
deboutant les autres comme mauvaises. Cellui de nature est

21. la Dieu grace tu n'as pas failli ains Dieux mercis
en a largement en pluseurs manieres et meismement plus communement autres dames n'ont les quelles choses *was crossed out*

because it is a great virtue not to wound whoever wounded you, and it is a great strength of heart not to return evil for evil, which are the things ordered by Our Lord in His Holy Gospel!"[6]

Here I speak of the fourth reason for consolation in   5
the death of friends, which concerns the friends who are
still alive, and of three principal gifts.

Now I will go back to our first subject on the reasons for consolation. The fourth reason which should comfort you, Revered Lady, is more pleasant since it concerns sensuality   10
and human frailty, which can barely do without the pleasures of this earth, and they are, to speak truly, not all completely vices, but permissible and honorable, and they do not displease God. Boethius put forth an argument in his
Book of Consolation which Philosophy, among other reasons   15
for consolation, proposed and offered to him when it reminded him of his children;[7] that is to say, there neither was nor is any creature so abandoned by all good fortune who does not to some degree, have reason for consolation--of this,
Very Noble Lady, by the grace of God, you are not deprived,   20
but, thank God, in some ways you have a great deal of it, even more than most ladies have--and not to recognize this would be an ingratitude, which is a grave sin. Therefore, your good heart should be aware of this, and remember in
thanking God for your consolation for the assaults and   25
wounds of tribulation when they affect you, the very large and noble benefits that you have received from your Creator, who wants you to use them well; and there are especially three from which many other goods come and on which they
depend, and these are: the gift of grace, the gift of   30
nature, and the gift of fortune.[8]

To understand better these three gifts, we have to know that two, when we have them, are inside us, and the third is outside. The one which is called grace is in the soul of
the human creature, and it is the one which gives under-   35
standing, as Aristotle says, to imagine and comprehend things that are or can be, to be able to comprehend and conceive things that one has seen, heard, or known, and to distinguish the ones from the others when one selects some
as good and rejects others as bad. The gift of nature   40

[6]Isidore, *Synonyma*, 2. [7]Boethius, *De consolatione philosophiae*, 2. [8]In Aristotle, *Ethica Eudemia*, 2.1.

ou corps, c'est assavoir: force, beauté, santé, habilité,
parole ordonnee, honnourable port, maniere arree, avenant
maintien, gracieuseté, et toutes telz choses qui au corps et
a ses mouvemens appartiennent. Le don de fortune sont
seigneurie, dominacion, puissance, richesces, noblece de 5
sang, bonnes aventures, avoir escheu a bonne et belle partie,
soit femme ou mary, belle ligniee d'enfans ou de haulx
parens, et toutes telz choses qui sont dehorz soy.

A revenir aux particularitez de quoy sert cellui don
d'entendement--le quel est et a sa situation ou chief--est a 10
savoir que de lui viennent et avecques lui demeurent .iii.
par especial moult nobles vertus. L'une est retentive,
l'autre memoire, et la tierce est raison. Retentive sert de
recevoir en soy les choses que l'entendement lui administre
et baille, si les retient. Memoire sert de ne laissier ou- 15
blier les choses retenues, ains les ramentoit et en donne
souvenance. Raison, qui est la tierce, euvre la voye de
mettre par effect a oeuvre ce que l'entendement a compris et
retentive a retenu et que memoire recorde. Raison, donques,
est l'administreresse de faire mettre a excecucion par oeuvre 20
si comme baillif ou prevost des mandemens du bon et sain entendement, comme il en soit d'uns et d'autres moult diffe-
renciez, et qui largement en a, n'est mie de petit tresor
enrichiz! Mais que bien en use, comme en ce monde ne soit
autre pareil. De ceste raison, vient et nait discrecion que 25
aucuns dient prudence, la quelle est si comme servante de
raison, et ses commandemens envoie et met es cuers des creatures, et distribue et depart tout ce qu'elle ordene. Ceste
discretion est dicte mere des vertus, la cause pourquoy est
ainsi appellee, est pour ce que la ou elles ne seroient 30
menees par elle, si que autrefois ailleurs ay dit, en vices
se convertiroient; si comme par exemple, largece est vertu,
mais non pour tant quant elle est excessive et trop et non
par discrecion menee, elle tourne en fole largece que on dit
prodigalité, la quel chose est vice. Item, devocion est 35
grant vertu et estre en oroison ou jeuner; neantmoins qui
tant y affoibliroit le corps et travailleroit que rompre lui
convenist et non continuer, ne seroit pas vertu.

Ce meismes dist Saint Jehan, et pour ce qui bien en
toute chose veult cheminer et faire bonnes oeuvres, convient 40
que soit par discrecion, la quelle est moienne entre le pou
et le trop; ceste vertu en creature la fait estre moult cler
voiant; c'est assavoir, avoir a memoire les choses passees
pour y prendre exemple devant les yeulx, celles a venir pour
y pourveoir, et les presentes pour les bien passer. Et pour 45
tant que sa proprieté est de faire loing et prés et environ
soy regarder, la personne discrete est en toutes choses

concerns the body, that is: strength, beauty, health,
methodical speech, honorable behavior, organized manners,
pleasant poise, grace, and all things relevant to the body
and its movements. The gift of fortune includes control,
domination, power, riches, nobility of blood, good outcomes, 5
to have found a good and beautiful spouse, be it husband or
wife; a beautiful lineage of children or high parentage, and
all similar things which are outside oneself.

To go back to the particular things for which the gift
of comprehension, which is and has its location in the head, 10
is used, we must know that three very special and noble virtues come from it and stay in it. One is retention, the
second memory, and the third is reason. Retention is used
to receive in oneself the things that comprehension controls
and entrusts to it, and then it retains them. Memory is 15
used in order not to forget things retained; it keeps and
reminds you of them. Reason, which is the third, opens the
way to put into practice what comprehension has understood
and retention has kept and what memory has recorded. Therefore, reason is the administrator of works--like a bailiff 20
or a provost marshal--of good and healthy comprehension,
since the latter can be very different in one man or another,
and whoever has a great deal of it, is enriched by no small
treasure! But he must make good use of it, because there
is none like it in this world. From reason comes and is 25
born discretion, which some call prudence, and like the
servant of reason, it sends off its orders to be put in the
hearts of men, and it distributes and imparts all that it
commands. This discretion is called the mother of all
virtues, and the reason why it is called this is because if 30
virtues were not under its command, as I said once in another
work, they would become vices; for example, generosity is a
virtue, but not when it is excessive and not checked by
discretion, for then it becomes a foolish generosity that we
call prodigality, which is a vice. Likewise, devotion, 35
prayers, and fasting are great virtues; nevertheless, if
someone weakens and overworks the body so much that it
breaks down and cannot continue, that would not be a virtue.

Saint John says the same: whoever wants to follow the
right path in everything and do good works has to do it with 40
discretion, which is the mean between too little and too
much; this virtue in a man makes him be very clear-sighted;
that is, he will keep in mind the things of the past to set
an example in front of his eyes, the things to come to provide for them, and the things of the present to live them 45
well. And inasmuch as the property of discretion is to make
one think far and near and around oneself, the discreet

avisee et pourvoit a tout selon son povoir; dont tout premierement comme au souverain bien, a regart a son ame et
pense de son salut, et pour ce, suit les voyes que Dieu
commande, et met paine du contraire eschever; de la quel
chose sourdent et naissent bonnes voulentez et desirs raison-   5
nables, des quelz ensuivent bonnes oeuvres; le corps aprés
avise a gouverner par tel discrecion qu'il demeure sain
d'onneur et de santé et a son povoir en convalescence tellement que tache n'y ait, ne reproche.

    Quant est aux susdis biens que nature donne, qui sont   10
ou corps, si que devant est dit, semblablement convient,
quelque habileté qu'il ait, que tout ainsi que au seigneur
appartient de gouverner sa gent, que par discrecion ilz
soient menez; autrement tout cherroit en foleur et en vice,
si comme par exemple de qui auroit beau langage mais tant   15
parleroit, que aux oyans tourneroit a ennuy et ainsi perdroit
sa loenge. Et dit un aucteur que de toutes choses bonnes,
le plus est le meilleur excepté de langage; pour ce, si que
dit est, y convient discrecion, qui amodere entre le trop
et le pou; si le fait bien a point, et adont est-il parfait   20
et trés bel; semblablement est d'autre abileté la demoustrer
et faire non en temps, ne en lieu, ne seroit de value et
ainsi des autres.

    Aux biens de fortune, qui est le .iiie. dessus dit don,
a les bien gouverner et sagement en user, n'y a pas pou   25
besoing d'ame discrecion, et la ou sans elle sont distri-
buez, tout tourne a folour et dommage; donques la personne
discrete, par bon avis, selon l'estat ou Dieu l'a appellee
et sa possibilité, se vouldra gouverner en chascune chose
tout au mieulx que faire se pourra; se d'Eglise est, vers   30
Dieu faire son devoir et ses biens distribuer aprés ses
neccessitez et convenable estat tenu aux povres, si que
faire le doit. Se mariez est, aviser et congnoistre les
condicions de sa partie; se bonnes sont, donner cause a
son povoir que continuees soient, et se mauvaises, trouver   35
voye, se on puet, de les amoderer, afin de vivre en paix
comme il ne soit plus grant enfer ou monde que riote en
mariage; se enfans a, leur donner bonne dottrine et aprendre
a craindre et servir Dieu; ne leur moustrer semblant en
jeunece de grant familiarité, ne trop amour, ains nourrir   40
en amoderee crainte, et les faire aprendre ou duire en la
science ou mestier que on leur veult donner. Se seigneur
est ou grant terrien a qui il appartiengne garde bien
justice, car c'est ce qui seingneurie maintient, par tel
discrecion gouverne ses subgiez qu'ilz le puissent aimer   45
[et] aussi doubter sagement; prendre garde a ses revenues
et tenir estat selon ce que elles sont--comme l'excessif et

person is knowledgeable in everything and sees to everything
as much as he can; first to the sovereign good, then he
considers his soul and his salvation, and to this goal, he
follows the ways ordered by God, and strives not to achieve
the opposite; from this come forth and are born good will   5
and sensible desires, which are followed by good actions;
after that, he tries to govern his body with such discretion
in order to stay full of honor and health, and puts so much
effort into staying healthy that he has neither blemish nor
cause for reproach.   10

As for the aforementioned goods that nature provides
and which concern the body, as was said previously, it is
truly proper that they be governed by discretion, however
one is capable of it, just as it befits the lord to rule
over his subjects so that they be led discreetly; otherwise,   15
everything would turn to folly and vice: for example, one
might possess beautiful speech, but would speak so much that
his listeners would be bored by it, and he would thus lose
his prestige. One author says that in all good things, more
is best, except for speech; it is said on that subject that   20
discretion must prevail, which moderates between too much
and too little; but if it is handled properly it is perfect
and very good; it is also good to show and present any other
ability, in time and in place; otherwise, it would not have
any value, and the same is true for others.   25

Concerning the goods of fortune, which is the third
gift mentioned above, to govern them and to use them wisely,
the soul needs not a little discretion, and where the goods
are distributed without it, everything turns to folly and
harm is done; therefore, the discreet person, with good   30
sense, according to the state that God called him to and
according to his own possibilities, will want to behave in
everything as best he can; if he is a man of the Church, he
will want to do his duty towards God and will give away the
riches he has left after he has used what he needs to insure   35
a decent condition for the poor, as should be done. If he
is married, he must consider and know what his spouse's
inclinations are; if they are good, he must exercise his
power to have them endure, and if they are bad, he must find
a way if he can to alleviate them so as to live in peace,   40
since there is no worse hell in the world than arguments in
marriage; if he has children, he must instruct them well
and teach them to fear and to serve God; he must not appear
too close to them when they are young, nor show too much
love, but raise them in a moderate fear, make them learn or   45
lead them into the sciences or the profession that he wants
to give them. If he is a lord or a rich landowner, who has

trop destruise souvent puissance et avoir de soy et
d'autrui--ne usurper l'autrui, ne soy souffrir oultre raison
fouler; si que dit Seneque, estre large en honneur selon son
estat et moustrer en meurs et en condicions et paroles,
maintiens et fais, que l'on soit noble si comme on y veult   5
estre appellez, l'estat rural et cotidien assez amoderé et
par ordonnance bonnes gens environ soy avoir et bien les
congnoistre, car si que dit Seneque: "Mieulx appartient au
sire congnoistre sa mesgniee que ce qu'ilz le congnoissent,
leur face du bien selon son povoir et tiengne honnestement,   10
faire bien aux bons et a ceulx qui le valent en les pour-
veant et pres de soy les tire." De faire bien aux bons, ma
redoubtee Dame, dist un moult beau mot ton excellent oncle,
le sage roy Charles, pere de cestui qui a present regne:
que il ne savoit en seigneurie ou richeces fors une seule   15
felicité et bien, c'estoit puissance de bien faire a autrui.
Et qu'il soit vray, sans faille, ceste liberalité est tant
noble que quant elle vient de bon courage, elle fait plus
joïeux en la faisant, cellui qui la fait que cil qui la
reçoit. Avec ce, donner aux povres pour l'amour de Dieu et   20
ne les grever, car ceste est l'espargne qui en sainte huche
se met pour le temps a venir, si ne doit estre plaint, car
mestier aura.

    Cestes manieres a tenir selon discrecion ou prudence
semblablement appartiennent selon leur qualité et estas   25
aux dames et autres dames differencieement, si que a
chascune appartient; et pareillement aux hommes, quoyque
plus largement se pourroit eslargir a dire sur ceste matiere
touchant chascun estat particulierement, mais pour briefté
a tant souffise la descripcion des susdis .iii. dons.   30

De ce meismes.

    Si que devant est touchié, ma trés redoubtee Dame, des-
susdis dons, me semble, et il est vray--a Dieu en soit la
loenge, et serviz et amez en puist-Il estre--qu'assez
souffisament tu en es douee. Je ne le dis, et, ce scet   35

    33. a Dieu en soit la loenge et serviz et amez en
puist-Il estre qu'assez souffisament tu en es douee je ne le
dis et ce scet Dieux pour toy flatter ne blandir ne donner
matiere d'avoir vaine gloire ains tout au contraire *was
crossed out*

to keep justice, since this is what maintains control, he
should rule over his subjects with such discretion that they
will love him and also fear him wisely; he should watch over
his revenues and live according to what they are--because
excess and prodigality often destroy power and one's and   5
others' riches--he should not usurp the riches of others, nor
allow damage to be caused beyond reason; as Seneca says,[9] he
should be generous with honors as befits his estate and show
in his mores, inclinations, speech, behavior, and actions
that he is as noble a man as he wants to be called; he should   10
keep in moderation the rural estate daily and by his command
keep a circle of good people around him and know them well,
just as Seneca says: "It is better for the lord to know his
household well than for them to know him, he must do good for
them and behave honestly, to do good things to good people,   15
and to those who are useful to him by providing for them and
drawing them to him."[10] Concerning doing good things for
good people, my Revered Lady, your excellent uncle, the wise
King Charles, father of the one who is now ruling, said an
excellent thing: that he knew of only one good in the state   20
of lordship and wealth, and that was the power to do good to
others.[1] And it is so completely true that this generosity
is so noble when it comes from a good heart, that it makes
the doer happier in so doing than the one who receives it.
With that, one should give to the poor for the love of God   25
and not harm them, because these are the savings put in the
holy cupboard for the time to come, and it should not be
lamented because there will be need for it.

         These examples of behaving according to discretion or
prudence apply in the same way to all the ladies according   30
to their various positions and estates in which each one is;
also to men, although I could say much more on that subject
and on each particular estate, but for the sake of brevity,
the description of the above three gifts will suffice.

         On the same subject.   35

         Concerning what I have said before on these gifts, my
Very Revered Lady, it seems to me and it is true--God be
praised for it, and may He be served and loved for it--that
you have received a good amount of them. I do not say that,

---

[9]In *De quatuor virtutibus cardinalibus.* [10]*Ibid.* [1]In
Christine de Pizan's *Livre des fais et bonnes meurs de sage
roy Charles V*, 3,29.

Dieux, pour toy flatter, ne blandir, ne donner matiere
d'avoir vaine gloire, ains tout au contraire, comme telz dons
ne soient mie choses qui de nous viengnent, mais viennent
de Dieu, dont tout ainsi que le servant qui de son seigneur a
receuz maints grans biens, graces et benefices, est plus   5
tenus de le bien servir, estre obeissant a ses commandemens,
se garder de le courroucier, estre plus humble, serviable
et bon de tant comme plus en a eu de biens, et plus seroit a
reprendre se le contraire faisoit, et plus devroit estre de
son maistre punis que cil qui tant n'en avoit receu, sembla-   10
blement est de creature humaine vers son Createur; et n'est
mie mal de congnoistre et sentir en soy, a creature qui l'a,
le bel entendement que on a receu de Dieu et le beau corps
fort, sain et puissant ou avenant, se on l'a, et la noblece,
richece ou grandeur ou l'en habonde; mais que ceste congnois-   15
sance ne soit mie en vaine gloire, ne en l'attribuant au
bien de soy meismes et que par ce, on se enorgueillisse:
tel chose est presompcion et pechié qui trop desplait a Dieu,
mais, se c'est en se reputant tant plus tenus a lui et plus
en doubte de faillir et que on en vaille mieulx en toutes   20
vertus, ce n'est fors tout bien, si comme meismement a autre
propos de ce que l'Euvangille dit, que ce que la main destre
donne ne sache la senestre, qui est a entendre que secretement soit faite l'aumosne. La cause pour quoy secretement
doit estre, c'est pour doubte que vaine gloire, qu'il   25
appelle la senestre, qui tant est soubtil pechié, par temp-
tacion d'ennemy de vouloir estre reputé bon, se fischat en
la personne qui publiquement la feroit, mais qui de ce
pechié bien se sauroit garder, et que on la feist pour donner
bon exemple a autrui de conforter les povres, mieulx seroit   30
la donner en publique et devant les gens qu'en secret. Et
semblablement est de peleriner et faire les oeuvres de
misericorde et tous autres biens, les quelles choses, par
especial a princes et princesses et toute puissant gent,
s'en entencion de donner bon exemple le font et sans vaine   35
gloire, sont de plus grant merite que a autres gens, pour
ce que occasion d'umilité et bien faire donnent. Et les
choses veues faire ou dire, soit bien ou mal, a grans
seigneurs ou dames, plus sont considerees et plus tournent
a exemple que d'autres personnes; et par ainsi, pues-tu   40
veoir que l'entencion juge l'omme; dont me semble que dire
puis sans mesprendre, et te ramentevoir pour ton reconfort,
les grans dons et graces que receues as de ton Createur qui
souffisans sont s'en toy ne tient de te mettre ou ciel aprés
ceste vie, mais que bien en uses et bien a vivre au monde;   45

The Prison of Human Life

God knows, to flatter you or to cajole you, or even to give
cause for vainglory, but just the opposite, since such gifts
are not things that come from us, they come from God, and
thus just like the servant who has received many great goods,
graces, and benefits from his lord is more bound to serve him 5
well, to obey his orders, to keep from angering him, to be
humbler, more useful and better as he has received more
liberalities and would be the wronger if he did do the
opposite, and should be punished more than the one who did
not receive as much, a human creature should be so towards 10
his Creator; it is not at all bad to know and to feel in
oneself, whoever has it, the beautiful intelligence that one
has received from God, the beautiful, strong, healthy, powerful, or handsome body, if one has it, and the nobility, richness, or grandeur where it is plentiful; but this knowledge 15
should not become vainglory, nor be attributed to one's own
value and by doing so, render one proud: such a thing is
presumption and sin which God dislikes very much, but it is
by wanting to be known to be so grateful to Him and so fear-
ful to fail that one is better in all virtues, which is all 20
good, as the Gospel also says for another purpose, that is,
that the left hand should not know what the right gives out,
meaning that alms should be given secretly.[2] The reason why
it should remain secret is for fear that vainglory, which
it calls the left hand, and which is a subtle sin, would 25
come into the person who would act publicly as he is tempted
by others to be known as a good man, but whoever could keep
himself from this sin, and would practice charity to give
as an example on how to comfort the poor, then he would do
better to do it publicly and in front of everyone than in 30
secret. Similarly, pilgrimages, works of charity, and other
good deeds, especially if princes, princesses, and all
powerful people do it with the intention of setting a good
example and without vainglory, are of greater merit for
them than for other people, because they give them the 35
chance to be humble and to do good. And the things, good
or bad, that one has seen or heard the great lords and
ladies do, are examined more closely and are more readily
followed than what other people do; therefore, you can see
that man is judged by his intentions; I can say that without 40
making a mistake, and I want to remind you for your own
consolation, of the great gifts and graces that you have
received from your Creator which are sufficient, if there is
in you something that wants to go to Heaven after this life;
but use them well to live well in this world; in these 45

[2]*Matthew* 6.3.

41

es quelles choses--louez en soit Dieux--t'a la susdicte
discrection si bien dottrinee que Renommee et ceulx qui te
congnoissent me dient le contraire que ainsi ne le faces et
tout vient de Dieu.

Aprés ces choses, les biens de fortune dont tu as   5
largement, sont-ilz a oublier? Et de quoy te plains?
N'es-tu de haulx parens, fille de filz de roy de France,
mariee hautement au bel et bon Jehan, duc de Bourbon? Mais
quelle est au monde plus grant joye aux mariez, par especial
haute gent, que avoir de beaulx enfans? Y as-tu donques   10
failli? Quoyque dire me pourroies que tes douleurs te ramen-
tois de ce dont ton cuer est en tristece, ne avoir ne puet
joye a cause de ton espoux et de ton ainsné filz, le conte de
Eu, par dure Fortune, si que dit est devant, en bien faisant,
en exposant leurs corps chevaleureusement pour leur souve-   15
rain seigneur et non par leur faulte, encheus es mains de
nos ennemis. Dieux, par Sa grace, tost les te ramaint a
joye, et tous les autres nobles François qui la sont! A ce
je te respons, ma redoubtee Dame, en repliquant ce que dit
est devant, que l'esperer en Dieu, en bien faisant pour eulx   20
et prendre en pacience, te puet empetrer grace envers Nostre
Seigneur de les bien tost ravoir, ce que Dieux tost te doint!
Et, quant a celle tribulacion, quoyque elle soit grant, elle
est meritoire, et la t'envoie Dieux afin que par les biens,
prosperitez et joyes ou tu habondoies en ce monde, ne te   25
feust tant plaisant qu'en oubliasses la voye d'aler ou
ciel, qui est ton droit heritage ou quel on ne puet aler,
selon que dit l'Escripture, par delices mondaines, ains par
le merite de patience, en tribula[cion] y convient passer.
D'autres beaux enfans assez n'as-tu, noble Dame? Bonne joye   30
t'en vueille envoier cil Dieu qui les a fais! C'est
assavoir: la bonne et belle ma Dame Bonne, contesse de
Nevers, quoyque moult la plaingnes et soies piteuse de sa
vesveté et dont en si jeunes jours perdi sa bonne partie,
[Phelippe], conte de Nevers, filz de Phelippe, duc de   35
Bourgoingne, filz et frere de roy de France, mort en la
susditte infortunee bataille; mais le sage et le bon gou-
vernement d'elle, non obstant le jeune aage, en la discrete
pourveance, nourreture et doctrine de ses nobles enfans et
des terres et seigneuries qui demourees lui sont, te rendra   40
de sa noble personne et sage maintien, consolee et joieuse.

1. es quelles choses louez en soit Dieux t'a la susdicte discrection si bien dottrinee que Renommee et ceulx
qui te congnoissent me dient le contraire que ainsi ne le
faces *was crossed out*   34. *blank space between* partie *and*
conte

matters--God be praised--the aforementioned discretion has
taught you so well that your renown and those who know you
tell me that you shall not do the opposite and that all
comes from God.

    After these things, should the gifts of fortune, of   5
which you have a great amount, be forgotten? Are you
complaining? Are you not of great lineage, daughter of the
King of France's son, married well to the beautiful and
good John, Duke of Bourbon? And is there a greater joy in
the world for married people, and especially for high people, 10
than to have beautiful children? Have you failed in this?
Although you could tell me that your sufferings remind you
that your heart is sad, and that you cannot have any joy
because of your spouse and your oldest son, the Count of Eu,
who, because of bad Fortune, as I said before, have fallen   15
into the hands of our enemies while they were doing well in
offering their bodies in a chivalrous manner for their
sovereign lord, and not by their own fault. May God, by
His grace, bring them back to you for your joy with all the
other French noblemen who are there! I will answer to you   20
on that subject, my Revered Lady, by saying what I already
said before, that hope in God, doing good for them, and being
patient, can obtain grace for you with Our Lord, so that He
may soon bring them back to you, may God give it to you soon!
And in regard to this tribulation, however great it is, it   25
is worthy, and God gives it to you so that the good things,
prosperities and joys of which you had plenty in this world
should not be so pleasant to you that you should forget
the way to go to Heaven, which is your right inheritance,
but to where one cannot go, as the Holy Scriptures say,   30
through worldly pleasures, but rather through the merit of
patience, and one has to go through tribulations. Do you
not have other beautiful children, Noble Lady? May God
who made them give you great joy with them! They are: the
good and beautiful Lady Bonne, Countess of Nevers, although 35
you pity her because of her widowhood; she lost in her
young years her good spouse Philip, Count of Nevers, son of
Philip, Duke of Burgundy, son and brother of the Kings of
France, who died in the aforementioned unfortunate battle;
but her wise and good behavior, in spite of her young age,   40
her discreet care, governance, and instruction of her noble

Semblablement, par la Dieu grace, pues attendre grant joye
de ton autre fille, ma Damoiselle [Catherine] de Bourbon, par
mariage encores, se Dieux plaist, hautement pourveue comme
bien le vaille; et se dire me veulx que la Fortune du temps
present trop mal s'i dispose, je te redis, ma Dame, ce que   5
devant est dit: que, se tu as en Dieu parfaite fiance, tu
verras Ses merveilles et Sa haute puissance sur toy et les
tiens en haux dons et graces descendre plus avant que penser
n'oseroies et le temps retourner en meilleur disposicion.
Mais que me diras-tu du surplus de ta belle porteure--que   10
je nomme au derrain tout de gré afin de te laissier meilleur
goust de joye, si comme les chiers et bons mes se donnent en
la fin--que Dieux, par Sa grace, te vueille sauver, sont-ilz
a oublier? Te est-ce pou de plaisir de veoir ce trés bel
jouvencel, Charles monseigneur, en si jeunes jours, comme   15
d'environ .xv. ans, tant bel, tant avenant et sage selon sa
jeunece, si vif, si appert et si gente personne de corps
et de viaire, que riens n'y deffault? Ou quel vraiement,
par belle dottrine et bon commencement, bien resplendit et
se moustre la haute et noble attraction dont il est venus!   20
Si ne forligne mie! Et l'enfançon Loys monseigneur? Quel
commencement a il, comme environ l'aage de .viii. ans se
demoustrer tant avenant, si congnoissant et de tant bon
entendement, si bel et si plaisant, quel tresor te puet-ce
estre? Certes, se en ce monde plus de richece et de biens   25
n'avoies que ces beaux enfans, si as-tu cause d'estre bien
joieuse, quoyque, sans faille, je sache assez que cuer qui
fort aime n'est point sans soussy de paour de perdre ce que
il a si chier. Dieux par Sa grace les te veuille sauver et
donner bonne joye!   30
    Et ainsi, ma redoubtee Dame, en concluant ce que devant
est dit, me semble et il est vray ces choses veues que
Dieu, nostre Createur, qui maintes creatures a fourmees a
son ymage aussi bien comme toy, et neantmoins des devant dis
.iii. biens et aussi des autres leur a ottroié en ce monde   35
petit ou neant, et que leur vie passent en maintes miseres
et grant povreté de santé et d'avoir, t'a donné de grans
dons. Regardes quel difference de toy a eulx! Se bien le
consideres, ce que je croy, que ton noble entendement ne le
mescongnoit mie! Or, est sans les autres trés haulx grans   40
biens ou tu habondes comme maints en y ait, si comme titre
de haute princesse, duchesse, renommee entre les plus grans,
habondant en honneurs, puissant en seigneurie et grant
terrienne et souffisamment aisiee en richesces, quoyque non

    2. *blank space between* Damoiselle *and* de Bourbon

children, her lands and properties which she has left, will
console you and make you happy in her noble person and wise
behavior. You may, by the grace of God, expect the same
great joy from your other daughter, the Lady Catherine of
Bourbon, who is still--if God grants it--highly married, 5
as she well deserves it;[3] and if you want me to say that the
Fortune of the present time is badly disposed to it, I will
say again, my Lady, what I said before: that, if you put a
perfect trust in God, you will see His marvels and His great
power shower upon you and your kin, His great gifts and 10
grace, much more than you ever dared think, and the time
return to a better disposition. But what will you tell me
of the rest of your beautiful children--whom I name last on
purpose so that you will have a better reason to rejoice,
just as the dear and good dishes are presented last--whom 15
God, by His grace, will spare for you, should they be
forgotten? Is it little pleasure for you to see this very
beautiful young man, my Lord Charles, in his young days,
about fifteen years old, so beautiful, so handsome and wise
in his youth, so quick, so open, so beautiful in the body 20
and face, that nothing is lacking? Truly, in him through
good upbringing and beginning, the high and noble beauty
where he came from shows and shines! Do not forget him!
And the child Lord Louis? What beginning he has, showing
himself at eight years of age, so beautiful, so well-taught 25
and intelligent, so handsome and so charming, is he not your
own treasure? Indeed, if you had not in this world other
goods and riches besides these beautiful children, you would
have cause to be very happy, although, undoubtedly, I know
well that a heart who loves much is not without the fear to 30
lose what it holds so dearly. May God by His grace spare
them for you and give you joy!
     Thus, my Revered Lady, to conclude what I said before,
it seems to me and it is true, after seeing these things,
that God, our Creator, who made you and many creatures to 35
His likeness, has nevertheless granted them little or none
of the three aforementioned gifts and others, and they spend
their lives in great miseries and serious lack of health and
riches, but He gave you great gifts. Look at the difference
between you and them! If you consider it well, which I 40
believe you do, let not your noble mind ignore it! And it
does not even include the other great goods that you have in
abundance; and they are many, such as the title of High
Princess and Duchess, renown among the greatest, abundance

[3]Catherine of Artois had married John of Bourbon, third
son of John I of Bourbon.

mie tant; et ce bien sçay-je que assez soit pour souffire a
ce que ton trés noble et liberal cuer vouldroit bien donner
aux bons, et bien faire a autrui qui seroit sans nombre.

Cy retourne au propos des bien morans.

Aprés ces choses dittes, ma trés redoubtee Dame, pour   5
revenir a la premiere matiere et traire a fin ceste present
oeuvre, comme assez souffisamment selon briefté soit demoustré es chapitres devant le premier parti des .ii. que au
commencement te mis au devant: le quel mieulx tu aimeroies
qui touche la misere de la prison de vie humaine et   10
caetera... Reste a declairer le second parti que je com-
paray a l'empire de tout le monde, ou quel est concluse la
.v^e. raison de l'appaisement du dueil que as de tes susdis
amis trespassez et autres tribulacions dont retourner me
convient au propos devant dit de ceulx qui bien sont mors,   15
c'est assavoir en grace; des quelz bien morans, soit en
bataille, en voyage, en pelerinage ou autre part, dit Saint
Augustin ou *Livre des confessions*, que ceulx qui crestiennement muurent en vraie foy comme catholiques confés, s'ilz
ont espace ou a tout le moins vrais repentans d'entencion et 20
desir de faire satisfacion s'ilz povoient, crians a Dieu
merci, que moiennant la misericorde de Dieu par le merite de
la passion Jhesu Crist, sont a sauveté et hors le peril de
dampnacion, quelque pecheurs que aient esté. Et dit oultre
que, quoyqu'ilz aient aprés ceste vie a souffrir paine, non   25
mie dampnable mais purgative, et l'un plus, l'autre moins,
selon la qualité des pechiez, ilz sont asseur de non estre
dampnez.
Dient les dotteurs de ces paines de purgatoire que elles
pevent estre, a ceulx qui y sont, abregiees par le moien   30
d'ausmones, oroisons, pelerinages et tous bienfais, la
quelle chose faire est souveraine charité et que oublier ne
doivent les amis vivans. O, tant sont eureux ceulx qui sont
hors de ce peril, quelque tourment qu'ilz aient, car au moins
ont-ilz le bien d'esperance qui les conforte de parvenir en   35
quelque temps a la joye qui ne fine et la consolacion d'estre
seurs de sauvement! Si n'est pas petite joye sans doubte
que grant refrigere et allegence donne aux tourmens souffers!
O, tant est de bonne heure nez qui ja est en celle glorieuse
compaignie, comme seurté y soit et non paour de l'orrible   40
sentence de dampnacion qui jamais n'est revoquee, de la
quelle nul vivant en ce monde ne puet estre aseur pour
l'abondance des pechiez ou souvent nous encheons et ne savons

in honors, power in lordship, wealth in land and possession
of a fair amount of wealth, although not a great amount; and
I know well that this is enough for your very noble and generous heart to want to give to good people, and do good to
others who are infinite in number.   5

Here I return to the subject of the men who died well.

After having said these things, my Very Revered Lady,
and to go back to my first topic and draw this work to a
conclusion, because I have discussed sufficiently though
briefly in the previous chapters the first of the two choices 10
which I proposed to you at the outset: which would you
prefer in regard to the misery of the prison of human life,
etc.... It remains to present the second choice that I compared to an empire for everyone, and in which is contained
the fifth reason for softening the grief that you feel for   15
the death of your aforementioned friends, and other tribulations which I want to discuss further, and namely the topic
of the men who died well, that is, with the grace of God;
and Saint Augustine in his *Book of Confessions* says about
these worthy men, dead in battle, or on a journey, on a   20
pilgrimage, or somewhere else, that those who die in true
faith, that is in the Catholic faith, if they have the time
or if they are at least truly repentant in intent and
willing to repent if they can, asking God for His mercy,
and with the mercy of God through the merit of Jesus Christ's   25
passion, they will be saved and free from the peril of
damnation, however sinful they may have been. And he adds
that, although they may have to suffer pain after this life,
a pain of purgation not of damnation, some more, others
less, according to the gravity of their sins, they are   30
assured of not being damned.
    The doctors say that these pains of purgatory, for
those who are in it, can be shortened by means of alms,
prayers, pilgrimages, and other good deeds, which are most
charitable things to do and not to be forgotten by the   35
living friends. Oh, how happy are those who are free of
this peril, however tormented they may be, because they have
at least hope which assures them to be able to go to the
endless joy and the consolation of being sure to be saved!
This great comfort and this relief do indeed give joy to the   40
ones who have suffered torments. Oh, how fortunate is the
one who is already in this glorious company, since there is
security in it, and there is no fear of the horrible sentence of damnation, which is never revoked, and of which
no living man can be sure, because of the many sins that we   45

l'eure de nostre fin, ne comment serons pris! Et Dieu dit:
"La ou je te trouveray, la te jugeray," qui est parole
moult a peser et trés redoutable; et pour ce dit bien la
Sainte Escripture: "Beneurez sont les mors qui muurent en
Nostre Seigneur;" le quel bien mourir, ce dit Boece, est   5
empetré par bien se congnoistre en pou prisant le corps,
comme il ne soit riens plus vil, et moult curer de l'ame,
comme il ne soit riens plus noble.

    A propos des bien mourans et contre ceulx qui les
pleurent, dit un aucteur, que plus digne est le jour de la   10
mort de creature humaine qui bien muert que le jour de la
naissance, et plus est esjoïssable, car dist-il, l'omme est
nez en pechié et perdus seroit, se sans la regeneracion et
lavement du baptesme mouroit. Mais aprés, se en aage de
discrection vient, il puet--se en lui ne tient morir en grace   15
et meismement tant de merite avoir acquis--qu'il va tout
droit ou ciel, si comme ont fait les benois sains. Le jour
de la naissance est l'entree en misere et tribulacion; le
jour de la fin, se bien muert, est l'issue de toutes afflit-
tions et miseres. L'omme est nez tout ignorant et sans   20
congnoissance, mais a la mort, congnoist mieulx Dieu que
onques, mais si se repent adont et merci crie, et par ce est
sauvez et ainsi va hors du peril ou tousjours a esté. Et
pour tant, dist-il, grant ignorance fait plourer et faulte
de foy aux amis qui plaignent les morz qu'ilz voient aler en   25
voie de sauvement. Et a dire, selon ce que aucuns usent de
langage, que quant on muert, on ne scet ou l'en va, est mal
dit et opinion et parole qui moult fait a reprendre, comme
nous ne soions pas cristiens ne dignes d'y estre appellez,
se nous foy n'avons et ferme creance en ce que la Sainte   30
Escripture nous certifie du sauvement ou dampnacion des ames
selon les fais, et commande a croire la foy et loy de Dieu.
Et quant est que ne le voions a l'oeil, si comme les folz
dient, ne riens n'en savons, fors ce que on nous donne a
entendre. Sans faille, creature qui en telle opinion se   35
fonde, ressemble ceulx qui ont trouble veue, qui faulses
medicines, pour la cuidier esclarcir, se mettent es yeulx, et
ainsi du tout s'avuglent. Semblablement telz doubtes a ceulx
qui les font, par ce que a l'oeil ne voient, les puet mettre
en l'avuglement d'erreur par trop investiguer et vouloir   40
enquerre; et ressemblent les Pharisiens, qui a Nostre
Seigneur demanderent a veoir signes, dont moult les redargua,
reprist et blasma, car dit la loy de Dieu que foy catholique
doit estre entierement, fermement et unement creue, ainsi

    30. nous *crossed out* foy n'avons

commit, and because we do not know the hour of our end, or
how we will die!, God says: "Wherever I find you, there you
will be judged;"[4] these are words to consider carefully and
to fear; and on this subject, the Holy Scriptures say:
"Blessed be those who die in Our Lord;"[5] Boethius says that   5
a good death can be gained by a good knowledge of one's self,
by despising the body, since there is nothing more vile, and
by a good care of the soul, since there is nothing more
noble.[6]

On the subject of those who have died well, and against   10
those who mourn them, an author says that the day of the
death of a human creature who dies well is of greater value
and joy than the day of his birth, since, he says, man was
born in a sinful state and would be lost, if he were to die
without the new life and cleansing given by baptism. But   15
afterwards, if he comes to the age of discretion, he can--if
he wants to die in grace and has thus acquired the necessary
merit--go directly to Heaven, just as the blessed saints have
done. The day of birth is the entrance into misery and
tribulation; the day of death, if one dies well, is the end   20
of all afflictions and miseries. Man was born ignorant,
without any knowledge, but when he dies, he knows God better
than ever, and if he repents and cries mercy, he is therefore saved and leaves the peril in which he had existed up to
that time. He says that total ignorance and lack of faith   25
make the friends who pity their dead cry, though they see
them go the path of salvation. To say, as some people do,
that one does not know where one is going after death, is
poor speech, poor words, and poor thinking, which are very
reprehensible, because we are not Christians or worthy to be   30
called Christians, if we do not have faith and firm belief in
what the Holy Scriptures say on the salvation or the damnation of souls according to their actions; and faith and the   `
law of God order us to believe in it. And whatever we cannot
see with our eyes, as the fools say, we cannot know, except   35
what is given to us to hear. Indeed, whoever believes such
reasoning, resembles those who have poor vision, and put the
wrong medicine in their eyes in order to clear them, and
thus become blind. Similarly, those who create these doubts,
because they cannot see, are in this erroneous blindness   40
because they search and want to ask too much; they are like
the Pharisees who asked Our Lord to see signs, for which He
shamed, corrected, and blamed them greatly, for the law of
God says that the Catholic faith must be entirely, firmly

[4]*Ezekiel*, 21.30. [5]*Revelation*, 14.13. [6]Boethius, *De
consolatione philosophiae*, 1.

comme nostre Sainte Mere Eglise le nous commande se estre
voulons participans ou merite que dit Jhesu Crist a Saint
Thomas: "Beneurez seront ceulx qui ne me verront et me
croiront."

Et qui plus est, pour approbacion de nostre foy, Platon   5
le philosophe, en son livre de *Phedron*, tout fust-il païen
et long temps avant l'establissement de la loy cristienne,
preuve par raison et moustre comment l'ame raisonnable par
bien faire doit aprés ceste vie avoir Paradis. Et dit
Prosper, en son livre *Epygramaçon*, qui aprés la mort, aux   10
bien mourans sera joye sans fin, lumiere sans tenebres,
voulenté toute, une santé sans maladie. Mais de celle
sainte cité de Paradis, dit Saint Gregoire, es *Morales* ou
.xxiiie. chapitre, que Dieux a demoustré le chemin aspre de
ceste vie, afin que les errans ne si delitassent tant que   15
ilz oubliassent par trop grant repos et joieux passage a
tenir la voie d'aler a leur droit païs qui est le ciel. Et
dit aprés: "Mais les cuers des esleus qui attendent les
grans joies de Paradis, prennent force contre les assaulx
des adversaires, car de tant comme plus croist la bataille,   20
de tant attendent-ilz plus glorieuse vittoire et tant que
si affermez sont es tribulacions que, si comme le feu ardant
dont le vent rabat la flamme si que il semble qu'il doie
estaindre, mais il le renforcist et le fait plus croistre,
ainsi par tribulacions croist leur ardeur de leur desir a   25
Dieu."

*Cy preuve par les dotteurs comment il n'est autre joye
que celle du ciel.*

Et ceste .v^e. et derraine conclusion qui est en la
seconde raison des .ii. parties devant proposees que je   30
assimilay a l'empire de tout le monde devant dit, quoyque la
comparoison ne soit, ne pourroit estre assez souffisant au
regard du mendre bien que recoivent les susdis desprisonnez
bien mourans--si comme par foy catholique le devons fermement
croire et ne devons de ce nullement doubter--si que dit est   35
et comme les sains dotteurs de l'Eglise le nous certifient,
ne n'est fors boe, ordure et neant toutes les joyes que
desirer ou souhaidier en cestui monde se pourroient envers
celles de la gloire celeste que recoivent en fin ceulx qui
bien trespassent; dont de ce disoit Boece, en la .iiii^e. part 40
de son livre: "O, vous mondains, qui naturelment desirez
souverain bien et qui tant vous penez a avoir aise, repos et

believed as one, just as our Holy Mother the Church orders
it from us, if we want to participate in the reward that
Jesus Christ described when He said to Saint Thomas:
"Blessed will be those who will not see me, and will believe
me."7   5
     Moreover, to confirm our faith, Plato the philosopher,
although he was a pagan who lived long before the establish-
ment of the Christian faith, proves by reason, and shows in
his book *Phaedo*, how the reasonable soul must gain Paradise
after this life of good actions. Prosper, in his book   10
Epigrammatum, says that, after death, those who died well
will know endless joy, darkless light, all desires, and an
illness-free health. But Saint Gregory says about this holy
City of Paradise, in the thirteenth chapter of the *Moralia*,
that God has presented the harsh path of this life, so that   15
the travelers do not enjoy themselves so much on it as to
forget, through great repose and happy journeying, to stay on
the road to their rightful land which is Heaven. And he
adds: "The hearts of the chosen which are expecting the
great joys of Paradise, gather strength against the assaults   20
of the enemies, because as the battle becomes harder, they
expect a more glorious victory, and they are made so much
firmer by tribulations that, just as the flame of a strong
fire is abated by the wind which seems to have to put it out,
in fact forces it back up and makes it stronger, through   25
their tribulations, their will to please God becomes
stronger."

     *Here the doctors prove that there is no other joy than
the one of Heaven.*

     This fifth and last conclusion which is in the second   30
reason of the two choices offered previously and which I said
was like an empire for everyone, although the comparison is
not, nor could be sufficient enough in regard to the smallest
joy received by the aforementioned freed men who died well--
as we must firmly believe it in our Catholic faith, and not   35
doubt at all--it is said, and the holy doctors of the Church
prove it to us, that all the joys that one could want or wish
in this world are nothing but mud, filth, and emptiness compared to those of the heavenly glory that those who die well
receive at the end; on that subject, Boethius said in the   40
fourth part of his book: "Oh, you worldly men, who naturally
desire the best of things, and who toil so much to reach
comfort, rest, and perfect happiness, you are indeed working

7*John* 20.29.

parfaite felicité, certes, en vain vous travailliez--dont
vous ressemblez a l'omme yvre qui toute jour quiert et trace
et retourner ne scet a son droit lieu--quant vous la querrez
en cestui monde ou elle n'est mie, mais eslevez voz yeulx
en hault et voz pensees adreciez a la beatitude sans fin et   5
la, trouverez parfait bien et toute felicité, comme le repos
des bien errans y soit; dont en cellui lieu fichiez les
regars de voz ymaginacions, car autre part n'a lieu de
souffissance. La est le secoure et refuge de tout labour,
consolacion, enterine beauté plus clere que le soulel, le   10
royaume eternel ou toutes choses sont assouvies, le quel
est promis aux bien mourans."
    Du quel dist l'Apostre, que comme nous n'aions point en
ce monde de demeure fors par emprunt, est nostre cité
pardurable ou ciel, de la quelle posseder devons singuliere-   15
ment curer comme de nostre perpetuel heritage. A ce propos
et que l'en doie avoir cure de l'acquerir et bien morir, dit
Quintilien, que tout ainsi comme l'omme prudent qui aler
doit en voiage se pourvoir de longue main de tout ce que
besoing lui est, doit le sage en ceste presente vie se pour-   20
veoir de bienfais comme plus il n'en emporte. Et adont, si
comme dit le philosophe Secondus, ne redoubtera la mort en
l'esperance de la paie de ses merites, moïennant grace Dieu,
car dit le Prophete, que les ames des mors en grace flouri-
ront comme la palme et vivront pardurablement. Et pour tant,   25
disoit bien Saint Augustin: "Tu, homme qui aimes richesces,
se amasser les veulz en lieu sauf et sans paour, fay ton
tresor ou ciel, car la est le grenier sans peril ou larrons
ne repairent, ne quelconques autre chose usurpant, ne
fortraiant, ne qui dommagier puist. Et se tu aimes honneur,   30
ou le vas-tu querant, que ou ciel ou quel lieu? Les non
dignes ne sont pas eslevez si comme ou siecle, car la est le
droiturier Distribueur qui les honneurs et merites depart a
chascun selon la dignité, si ne te y pourra nul faire tort
de ton loier. Se tu as chiere ta santé et maladie ou   35
viellece, ressongnes, ou la quiers-tu? Ne mais ou ciel ou
n'a maladie, n'enfermeté quelconques, n'aucune dueillance.
Meismement mort n'y a que veoir, ains toutes choses y vivent
et sont en prosperité; dont, se longue vie desires quier la,
celle pert, car ailleurs ne la trouveras."   40

in vain--and you look like the drunken man who looks everywhere all day long, searches, and cannot find his proper
place--when you search for them in this world where they are
not, lift up your eyes and turn to the endless blessedness,
and there you will find the perfect good and all happiness, 5
because there is the repose of the worthy travelers; therefore keep the aim of your thoughts on this place, because
nowhere else is comparable to it. There you will find assis-
tance and refuge from travail, consolation, a total beauty
more brilliant than the sun, the eternal kingdom where all 10
things are accomplished, and which is promised to those who
die well."[8]

On this subject, the Apostle says that, just as we do
not have in this world an abode, except for a borrowed one,
our City in Heaven is eternal, and we should work hard to 15
take possession of it, since it is our perpetual heritage.
Quintilian says on the subject of working and dying well
that, just as the prudent man who must go on a journey must
provide for himself very early all that he will need, so must
the wise man in this present life provide himself with as 20
many good deeds as he can take with him.[9] Therefore, says
the philosopher Secondus, this man will not fear death hoping
to see his merits rewarded with God's help, because the
Prophet says that the souls of those who died in grace will
blossom like the palm and live forever. Saint Augustine says 25
on this: "You who like riches, if you want to gather them in
a safe and secure place, put your treasures in Heaven, for
this is the danger-free loft where no thief can come in, or
steal anything, or rob, or do any damage. And if you like
honor, where will you find it, in Heaven or in some other 30
place? The unworthy will not be elevated as in this world,
because there is the fair Distributor who has imparted honors
and merits to all according to their worth, and He can make
no mistake about your reward. If you care about your health,
and sickness, and old age, think, where will you seek them? 35
Not in Heaven, where there is no sickness, nor any infirmity,
nor any grief. Nor is death seen there; all things live and
prosper; therefore, if you wish to seek long life there, let
this one go, for you won't find it anywhere else."[10]

[8]In *De consolatione philosophiae.* [9]Quintilian,
Institutio oratoria. [10]In *De Civitate Dei.*

Cy dit des joyes de Paradis.

Encores restes a regarder en conclusion se pourrons a
souffissance trouver escriptures tesmoingnables des grans
joyes de Paradis, a l'equipolant et similitude a l'empire
de tout le monde, ou toutes joyes mondaines a droit souhaid   5
feussent a cellui qui le possederoit accomplies; et de ce,
pour l'amour de toy, ma très redoubtee Dame, me suis encore
très bien enquise es livres des benois dotteurs de Sainte
Eglise que j'ay en ceste matiere diligemment cerchiez, es
quelz ay trouvé monseigneur Saint Augustin ainsi disant: 10
"Ou est l'entendement d'omme mortel assez souffisans pour
comprendre l'inconscriptible habondance de gloire qui est en
celle benoite cité de paradis, de la quelle exprimer a son
droit ne souffiroient toutes les langues de mortelz, ne les
yeulx aviser, ne oreilles entendre la beatitude que ont les   15
glorieuses ames sauvees?" Et pour ce, Saint Gregoire en son
Omelie dit ainsi: "Se nous bien considerons quelles et
combien grandes choses nous sont promises es cielz, nous
reputerons neant et viles toutes les plus grans joies,
honneurs et aises que avoir pourrions en cestui [monde], ne   20
toutes les prosperitez temporelles envers la vie eternele
sont chetiveté et mort, car cellui Dieu, qui est seul souverain bien et dont tout autre vient et depent, a voulu
qu'en sa benoite et infinie gloire soient participans ceulx
qui a lui sont alez et vont par le chemin qu'il a ordené, la   25
quelle gloire--tout ainsi que de la fontaine saillent et
viennent les ruisseaulx des yaues--ist la beatitude, qui a
tous les beneurez se depart et estent, qui est tant grande
seulement en remirant celle très glorieuse et benoite deïté,
qu'ilz sont assouvis de toutes joyes et ont ataint la sou-   30
veraine et parfaite felicité et accompli bien; ne plus ne
vouldroient, ne souhaidier ne saroient."
"O, quel gloire incomprenable a nostre congnoissance et
rude entendement qui en cestui monde ne le puet proprement
sentir," dist Saint Augustin, "veoir face a face la Benoite   35
Trinité, la sentir, assavourer et comprendre, estre en celle
glorieuse celeste compaingnie; veoir la glorieuse Vierge
Marie a la dextre de son filz essauciee et eslevee sur toute
autre creature en gloire merveilleuse, belle plus que ymaginer ne se pourroit; congnoistre et veoir la belle   40
ordonnance des cieulx et des choses qu'ilz contiennent, estre

10. Augustine *in margin* 37. compaig *crossed out*
celeste compaingnie

Here I talk of the joys of Paradise.

It remains to consider in conclusion if we can find
testimony in the Scriptures of the joys of Paradise, equiva-
lent or similar to everyone's empire, where all worldly joys
that one would wish could materialize; and for this, and for   5
your love, my Very Revered Lady, I have inquired a great deal
into the books of the blessed doctors of the Holy Church,
which I have searched through very diligently for that purpose, and I found the Lord Saint Augustine who said: "Where
is enough understanding in a mortal man to grasp the inde-   10
scribable abundance of glory that is in this blessed City of
Paradise, which all mortal tongues could not suffice to
explain fully, nor the eyes to see, nor the ears to hear the
blessedness which the glorious saved souls have acquired?"[1]
Saint Gregory says in his *Homelia*: "If we consider which and   15
how great the things promised to us in Heaven are, we will
hold as naught and vile all the greatest joys, honors, and
comforts that we could have in this world, all the temporal
prosperities are but misery and death compared to eternal
life, because this God, who alone is the sovereign good and   20
from whom all other goods come and on whom they depend, has
wished that those who have gone to Him, and gone the way He
has ordered, participate in His blessed and infinite glory,
and from this glory--just as the streams gush forth and flow
from the fountain--come blessedness, which is imparted and   25
remains in all the blessed, and it is so great only by the
simple reflection of this very glorious and blessed deity,
that all their joys are satisfied, and they have the sovereign and perfect happiness and realized goodness; they do
not wish for anything more, nor are even able to."   30
"Oh, what glory, incomprehensible to our knowledge and
crude understanding which cannot grasp it properly in this
world," says Saint Augustine, "it is to be face to face with
the Holy Trinity, to feel it, to savor and understand it,
to be in this glorious heavenly company; to see the glorious   35
Virgin Mary on the right of Her son, fulfilled and elevated
above all other creatures in a marvelous glory, more
beautiful than can be imagined; to know and to see the
beautiful order of the Heavens and of the things contained
therein, to witness the hierarchies and orders of the blessed   40
angels, archangels, cherubim and seraphim, thrones and

[1]*Ibid.*

presens aux ierarchies et ordres de benois anges, archanges,
cherubins et seraphins, thrones et dominacions; veoir leurs
offices et degrez, oïr la doulce melodie de leurs chans,
louent Dieu incessamment, plus accordable que autre quelconques musique souefve et delittable sur toute chose; estre   5
entre eulx par degrez selon le merite d'un chascun, sans
envie avoir l'un sur l'autre, mais en parfaite charité, amour
et dilettion et assouvie suffisance; veoir la gloire des
benois apostres euvangelistes, martirs et confesseurs et de
ces belles vierges chantans devant Dieu et tous sains et   10
saintes; veoir les benoites ames sauvees souvent et menu
arriver ou ciel," si que dit cellui meismes Saint Augustin,
"purgiees des pechiez, menees par les anges, la glorieusement
receues a grant feste et joye de toute la court de Paradis;
estre repeus de pardurable joye tant glorieuse et parfaite   15
que saouler n'en muer on ne s'en porroit, ains de plus en
plus amable et desirable, sans mendier, mais a largece, et
sans en avoir souffreté. Et pour tant," disoit-il, "onques
yeux ne virent, n'oreilles n'oïrent, ne cuers ne porent
comprendre biens pareilz a ceulx que Dieux a apprestez a ses   20
bons amis."

     Et de ce dit Saint Bernart en un sermon: "O, quel
beatitude, se mirer en celle eternelle resplendeur de la
Benoite Trinité ou joye pardurable est comprise, souffissance
enterine, richece et habondance de tous delices a comble et   25
droit souhaid; leesce plus grande que on ne pourroit comprendre et de toutes pars ne veoir, n'oïr fors toute parfaite
joye, non mie la joye qui vient de creature, mais du
Createur, qui estre ne puet tollue; au regart de la quelle
toute autre n'est fors tristece, tout autre souefveté est   30
douleur, tout autre doulceur est amertume, tout autre beauté
est laidure, et ensurquetout, toute autre riens qui delitter
puist, n'est fors chose moleste, empeschable et vaine envers
ceste gloire! O, les folz musars aucuns, qui par jeunece,
folie ou par cuider estre au monde en aucune prosperité,   35
dient qu'ilz vouldroient que Dieux gardast son Paradis et a
tousjours vivre ça jus les laissast! Cestes, ils ressemblent aux porcs, les quelz pour tous delices eslisent le
fiens et la boe et la se voultrent et enveloppent. Dieux,
quel ignorance, avuglement et faulte de soy: estre hors des   40
dangiers de fain, de soif, de froit, de povreté, de maladie,
d'avoir sa vie [hors] de tout courroux, d'inconvenient, des
tours de Fortune, estre aseur de jamais ne morir et [hors]
de toutes choses qui pevent troubler et nuire, et avoir
certaineté de perpetuelment demourer en gloire sans jamais   45

dominations; to see their offices and ranks, to hear the soft
melody of their songs which praise God incessantly, a music
more harmonious than any other, soft and delightful in every
way; to be with them by rank according to one's own merit,
without envying others, but to be in perfect charity, love,   5
affection and be well satisfied; to see the glory of the
blessed apostles and evangelists, martyrs and confessors, of
the beautiful virgins singing in front of God and all the
saints; to see the blessed saved souls arrive frequently and
quickly to Heaven," as Saint Augustine himself says, "purged   10
from sins, led by the angels, and there gloriously welcomed
with great joy by the entire court of Paradise; to be nour-
ished with such eternal, glorious, and perfect joy that one
could not have enough of it or replace it; to like and to desire it more and more, not begging but receiving it largely,   15
and without having to suffer for it. However," he says, "no
eyes have seen, no ears have heard, no hearts can understand
the good things that God has reserved for His good friends."[2]
     Saint Bernard says on that subject in a sermon: "Oh,
what a blessedness it is to see oneself in this eternal   20
splendor of the Holy Trinity where perpetual joy inheres,
complete satisfaction, richness, and abundance of all
delights beyond every wish; there is a happiness greater than
the mind can conceive or see anywhere else, only perfect joy
can be heard, not the joy which comes from a human, but from   25
the Creator, and it cannot be taken away; compared to it,
everything else is sadness, all other delight is grief, all
other sweetness is bitterness, all other beauty is ugliness,
and above all, any other thing that could delight is just a
vile, reprehensible and vain thing compared to this glory!   30
Oh, the ignorant fools who say, because they are young,
stupid, or because they think they are to prosper in this
world, that they would want God to keep His Paradise and to
let them live down there forever! Indeed, they resemble the
pigs, who select for their delights the slime and the mud,   35
roll in them, and cover themselves with them. God, what
ignorance, blindness, and self-created mistake: to be out
of the perils of hunger, thirst, cold, poverty, illness, to
lead one's life without anger, inconveniences, bad turns of
Fortune, to be sure never to die, and be free from all   40
things that trouble and harm, and to be certain to remain in
eternal glory without leaving ever! Oh, are there such and
similar gifts down there--they never were with the happiest
men, and they will never be!"
     The difference is too great, and as Saint Gregory says: 45

[2]*Ibid.*

partir! O, quelz dons sont-ilz ça en bas telz ou pareilz,
meismes aux plus eureux onques ne fu, a nul jamais ne sera!"

Trop y a a difference, car dit Saint Gregoire: "Ou
devons-nous querre la vertu de paix ne mais ou ciel, ou quel
lieu, au contraire de ce bas monde celle glorieuse com-   5
paingnie ou n'a envie, s'esjoïst de la beneurté l'un de
l'autre tellement que la gloire des uns redonde et reflechist
es autres qui leur est accroissement de gloire par union
conjointe qui estre ne puet separee, dont ensemble ilz
s'esjoïssent, louant Dieu." Et dist Saint Anseaume, qu'en   10
toutes choses comme roys, ilz ont puissance et auttorité a
leur plaine voulenté, car dist-il, tout ainsi comme Dieu
peut ce qui Lui plaist par Soy-meismes, ils pevent tout ce
qu'ilz veulent par ycellui Dieu a qui ilz sont conjoins.
Et dit oultre, que Dieux a ouvert ses grans tresors aux   15
beneurez et tout abandonné, et pour ce sont a eulx toutes
honneurs, delices et richeces et non a autres, car le Sauveur
les a fais tresoriers, seigneurs et gouverneurs comme ses
propres filz et heritiers a perpetuité, ou quel plus ilz
s'esjoïssent de la gloire de Lui-meismes que de leur meismes   20
beatitude, et autant de celle de leurs prouchains comme de la
leur propre. A ce propos, en parlant a yceux beneurez,
disoit le Prophete: "Vous estes tous Dieux," voire, par
grace, vouloit-il dire, en tant qu'ilz sont fichiez en Lui et
Lui en eulx, pour ce sont une meismes chose. Et ainsi de-   25
meurent habondans en infinis biens, plus que ymaginer ne se
pouroit en toute sapience, sachans toutes sciences. Et pour
tant, sont bien conseilliees toutes les creatures de ce monde
quant en leurs necessitez se tournent vers les benois sains
et saintes, priant devotement que intercesseurs leur soient   30
vers Nostre Seigneur.

*Cy dit de la gloire des beneurez aprés le jour du
Jugement.*

Dient les Sains Escrips, que au jour de Jugement, tous
corps recevront leurs ames et resusciteront; dont par divine   35
sentence, les beneurez iront a dextre et les dampnez a
senestre, selon d'un chascun les merites ou les meffais, si
que dit l'Euvangille. Quant des chetifs, pour ce que ma
matiere ne requiert parler des paines qui leur sont deues,
ne entrepris ne l'ay, quoyque les dotteurs, Job et mains   40
autres les dient estre infiniement horribles, si comme je le
tiens fermement--dont de celle compaingnie nous gart Dieux

28. toutes *crossed out* les creatures

"Where should we look for the virtue of peace but in Heaven,
in which place, contrary to this world down here where this
glorious company does not want to be, everyone enjoys so
much each other's blessedness, that the glory of some
abounds and is reflected unto others which augments their   5
glory through a tight unity which cannot be separated, and
together they rejoice while praising God." Saint Anselm
says that they have, like kings, all power and authority to
their full will, for, he says, just as God can do what He
likes by Himself, they can do all that they want through God   10
to whom they are united. And he also says that God has
presented His great treasures to the blessed, and given up
all of it to them, and thus all honors, delights, and riches
are theirs, and not others'; for God has made them trea-
surers, lords, and governors as well as His own sons and   15
heirs in perpetuity, for which they rejoice, more over His
own glory than over their blessedness, and more over the
others' blessedness than their own.[3] On this subject, and
speaking to the blessed, the Prophet says: "You are all
God," that is, he meant, by grace, in as much as they are   20
placed in Him, and He in them, since this is the same thing.
Thus they remain in an infinite abundance of goods, more than
all knowledge, including all sciences, could know. And for
that, all the creatures of this world are well advised when
in need, to turn towards the blessed saints, devoutly   25
praying them to be their intercessors with Our Lord.

*Here I speak of the glory of the blessed after Judgment
Day.*

The Holy Scriptures say that on Judgment Day, all the
bodies will receive their souls and rise again; by divine   30
judgment, the blessed will go to the right, and the damned
to the left, according to one's merits or misdeeds, as the
Gospel says.[4] As for the wretched, because my subject
does not require that I speak of the pains that are due to
them, nor have I done so, although the doctors, Job, and   35
many others say that they are infinitely horrible, and I
believe it--may God keep us from this company, and may we

[3]In *Proslogium seu alloquium de Dei existentia*, 25.
[4]*Matthew* 25.33.

et nous meismes garder du desservir nous puissons--n'en
pense en ceste present oeuvre riens traictier. Des beneurez
dient que avec leur juge Jhesu Crist iront en Paradis,
d'ycelle benoite procession peussions-nous estre! La gloire
que auront ces benois corps resuscitez, sera en accroissement   5
de la beatitude precedant que les ames avoient, dont entre
les autres gloires et joyes, en mettent .xii. que ilz
figurent a une couronne d'autant de luisans estoilles en
lieu de pierres precieuses qui a un chascun comme roy et
vittorieux, sera mise sur son chief.   10
     La premiere estoille est la joye que le corps, qui
naturelment aime l'ame, et l'ame qui semblablement aime son
corps, aura d'estre conjoint glorieusement sans jamais partir
avec celle qu'il a tant amee, dont mort l'avoit separé et
elle, de veoir son compaignon le corps, sauvé avec elle. La   15
.iie. estoille est que yceulx corps glorifiez verront des
yeulx corporels, ainsi comme le benoit Job le prophetisa, la
glorieuse humanité de Jhesu Crist en Sa magesté, glorieusement costé Son pere, a qui se verront semblables quant a
l'umanité, et du quel seront embraciez et conjois comme   20
freres par creacion. La tierce que ilz se trouveront fors
legiers et puissans en jeunece comme en l'aage de .xxx. ans,
parfais de tous menbres, quelque difformité ou laidure que
aient eu au monde, tant beaux, clers, nets et reluisans que
ilz passeront la beauté du soleil qui meismement sera .vii.   25
fois plus resplendissant que ore n'est, et la lune comme le
soulleil; et seront tant precieux que ilz rendront odeur et
soueftume savoureuse plus plaisant que le basme ne quelconques autre odeur.
     La quarte est la joye de ce que ilz se sentiront des-   30
pouillez et desnuez de celle ignorance, rudece et pesanteur
terrestre que avoir au monde souloient qui, non sachans, les
tenoit rustiques et enfermes; et ilz se trouveront avoir
parfaite sapience, sachans toutes sciences, congnoissans
toutes choses parfaitement, sentir l'infinie bonté de Dieu,   35
le quel ils verront assistamment, recongnoissant la grant
grace que de Lui ont receue, qui dignes les a fais d'estre
de celle glorieuse compaignie, dont de leurs propres langues,
les mains jointes, en donnant voix melodieuses, Le be-
neistront et loueront incessamment. La .v^e., que ilz verront   40
et congnoistront leurs peres et meres, mary, femme et enfans
et tous parens et amis; se sauvez sont, s'esjoïront de leur
gloire; se dampnez sont, seront contens de la justice de
Dieu, car le plaisir de Lui ne leur pourroit desplaire, ne
nulle chose troubler. Si parleront ensemble, car ilz auront   45

     15. avec el *crossed out* sauvé avec elle

keep from deserving it--I do not think that I will say anything in this present work. It is said that the blessed
will go to Paradise with their judge Jesus Christ, and may
we be in this holy procession! The glory that will befall
these blessed, resurrected bodies will augment the blessed-   5
ness that their souls already had, and among all the other
glories and joys, there are twelve which will be placed in
a crown of as many shining stars in place of precious stones,
and which will be placed on the head of each as king and
victor.   10
    The first star is the joy that the body, which naturally
loves the soul, the soul likewise loving its body, will feel
in being gloriously united with what it had loved so much,
but from which it had been separated by death, and which
the soul will have to see its companion, the body, saved with   15
it. The second star is that these glorified bodies will see
with corporeal eyes, as the blessed Job prophesized it,[5] the
glorious humanity of Jesus Christ in His majesty, standing
gloriously near His Father, they will see themselves like
Him in humanity, and they will be embraced by Him and united   20
as brothers in creation. The third is that they will find
themselves slender and powerful at the youthful age of
thirty, with perfect limbs, whatever deformity or ugliness
they had on earth, so beautiful, luminous, sharp and splen-
did, that they will surpass the beauty of the sun which will   25
itself be seven times more resplendent than it is now, and
the moon like the sun; and they will be so rare that they
will give off a scent and a delicate perfume more pleasant
than balm or any other odor.
    The fourth is the joy that they will feel to be free   30
and rid of the earthly ignorance, coarseness and weight
that they had in this world which, in their unknown state,
kept them boorish and loathsome; they will find that they
have all forms of knowledge, know all things perfectly,
feel the infinite goodness of God, whom they will see every-   35
where, recognizing the great grace that they have received
from Him, and which made them be of this glorious company,
and with their own tongues in melodious voices, and joined
hands, they will bless and praise Him incessantly. The
fifth is that they will see and know their fathers and   40
mothers, husband, wife, and children, and all kin and
friends; if these are saved, they will rejoice over their
glory; if they are damned, they will be satisfied with God's
justice, for His pleasure could not displease them nor
spoil anything. They will speak together, because they will   45

[5]*Job* 27.

memoire, souvenir et congnoissance, sans ignorance ne oblivion de toutes choses passees, et sauront tout quanque eulx
et autres onques firent, et tous les biens et tous les
maulx, non mie en honte mes se conjoïront entre eulx, si
comme l'amy s'esjoïst de son amy quant eschapez le voit d'un   5
grant peril. Et loeront Dieu, dont grace leur a faite, que
repentis et retrais se sont de leur pechiez, par quoy ilz
sont sauvez.

La .vi^e. que leur benoit corps glorifié sentiront, tant
agile, mouvant, sain et legier--non obstant la solideté et   10
espesseur du corps et membres--que partout ou il leur plaira,
pourront passer et entrer sans ouverture faire; dont quant
a plaisir leur vendra par maniere de soulas, pourront eulx
transporter en cestui monde qui adont sera modifié et la
terre toute consommee par feu, si que le dit la Sainte   15
Escripture, et fait net de toute ordure, plus cler et
transparant que cristal, et fait bel et delittable mer-
veilleusement, si iront du ciel ou monde a leur plaisir sans
se parer de leur gloire, ne de riens l'amendrir, ne de la
vision de Dieu. La .viie., que ilz se esjoïront en ce que   20
au contraire de ce qu'ilz souloient veoir au monde, se
trouveront ou lieu ou toutes vertus, et non autre part, sont
colloquees, et assises toute felicité et beatitude, si comme
par les sains dotteurs leur avoit esté dit plus C^m millions
de foiz, que comprendre, n'ymaginer n'eussent sceu, si comme: 25
bonté et sainteté, enterine dottrine, paix, verité, justice,
raison, force, liberalité, charité, amour, sapience, seurté,
liberté, beatitude, sainte vie, immortalité, grace, joye,
pitié, dilection, honneur, puissance, honneste compaignie,
vittoire, dignité, equité, amitié, beauté, triumphe, loenge,   30
magesté, gloire, souveraineté, plenitude de tous biens plus
que ymaginé ne porroit estre, dont ilz joïront a perpetuité.

La .viiie. sera la trés grant consolacion que ilz
prenront l'un avec l'autre, eulx voiant si belle compaignie
de sauvez en ames et corps humains portans lumiere, ou riens   35
n'aura de lait ne vergongneux, mais apperra tout bel quanque
Dieux a fourmé sur corps d'omme et de femme lors que
penitance aura tout purgié et nettoié; ce qui souloit estre
apte et prompt a pechié sera converti en lumiere et beauté
sans comparoison, plus pure qu'en l'estat de la premiere   40
innocence ou furent fourmez Adam et Eve, nos premiers
parens, n'estoient ains que pechié eussent. La .ixe. est la
trés grant joye et consolacion que ilz prendront en la

4. mes *was in margin*   22. sont *crossed out* et non
autre part   40. la premiere innocence *crossed out* l'estast
de la premiere innocence

have memory, recollection, and knowledge, no ignorance nor
oblivion of all the past things, and they will know all that
they and others did, all the good and bad things, not feel
shame but joy among themselves, just as a friend rejoices
to see his friend having escaped from a great danger. They   5
will praise God, who gave them His grace to have repented
and redeemed their sins, and by which they are saved.

The sixth is that they will feel their blessed and
glorified body, so agile, nimble, healthy and light--in spite
of the substantiality and thickness of it and its limbs--that   10
they will be able to go anywhere they please without the need
of openings; and whenever they will want, as a matter of
pleasure, to transport themselves in this world which will
be changed, while on earth all is consumed by fire, as the
Holy Scriptures say, and rid of all slime, clearer and more   15
transparent than crystal, made beautiful and marvelously
delectable, then they will go from Heaven to earth as they
please, without the ornament of their glory, but without
lessening it or the vision of God in any way. The seventh
is that they will rejoice in that, contrary to what they   20
were used to seeing in the world, they will be in the place,
and no other, where all virtues are gathered, and where
all felicity and blessedness have their place, just as it
had been told to them more than a hundred thousand million
times by the holy doctors, but which they could neither   25
understand nor imagine--virtues such as: goodness and
holiness, complete doctrine, peace, truth, justice, reason,
force, liberality, charity, love, wisdom, security, liberty,
blessedness, holy life, immortality, grace, joy, pity,
pleasure, honor, power, honest company, victory, dignity,   30
equality, friendship, beauty, triumph, praise, majesty,
glory, sovereignity, a plenitude of goods more than could be
imagined, and which they will enjoy forever.

The eighth will be the great consolation that each one
will feel for one another, seeing such beautiful, shining   35
company of saved souls and human bodies, in which nothing
will be ugly nor shameful, but everything that God has
formed on the body of a man and a woman will appear beautiful, after penance has purged and cleansed everything; what
was apt and ready for sin will be transformed into peerless   40
light and beauty, purer than the state of the first innocence was, when Adam and Eve, our first parents, were
formed, before they sinned. The ninth is the very great joy

parfaite paix, amour et union qu'ilz auront l'un avec l'autre
et ou bien qu'ilz se verront entre avoir Jhesu Crist;
aimeront Dieu parfaitement pour la bonté de Lui, leurs prouchains pour l'amour de Dieu, tous d'une voulenté et concorde,
comme ung corps, une Eglise triumphant, espouse de Dieu,   5
environ le quel ilz seront comme Son peuple, quoyque soit en
plus hault degré l'un que l'autre selon les merites, mais
tous en auront largement sans envie, mais chascun a souffisance; leur roy Jhesu Crist verront en Son throne, qui les
aimera, ainsi comme Il dit en Son Euvangille qu'Il est le   10
bon pastour qui congnoist Ses ouailles, pour les quelles Il
se est exposé pour les tollir a leur adversaire.
    La .x^e. estoille est la trés grant incomprenable joye
que ilz auront de ce que tant amez et cheris se verront de
leur Createur, Dieu le pere, qui les traittera comme filz   15
de Jhesu Crist qui les reputera comme freres, qui tant haulx
dons leur aura donnez et de parfaites graces; de ce parleront
ensemble en eulx entre esjoïssant, Le recongnoissant comme
pere qui fais les aura coheritiers de Son benoit royaume
et infinie gloire. La .xie. sera la parfaite leesce et   20
trés grant plaisir qu'ilz prendront en--trés parfaitement,
ains de toute leur puissance--celle Benoite Trinité qui
est un seul Dieu, ou quel tant seront fichiez par ardant
affection pour l'infinie bonté de Lui, que ilz ardront
d'affection amoureuse, pensant les biens que ilz en auront   25
receus tellement, que de celle dilection seront tous embeuz
et comme enyvrez, cogitant comment Dieu le Pere daingna
envoier Son filz en terre pour eulx prendre char humaine,
Dieu le Filz, la seconde personne de la Trinité, se ombrer
en la Vierge Marie et prendre corps humain, le benoit   30
Jhesu Crist, le quel souffri tant amere mort pour les rache-
ter des paines ou ilz estoient encheus par la faulte des
premiers parens; Dieu le Saint Esperit, qui tellement les
aura enluminez que de pechié se seront retrais et repentis,
par le quel moien seront parvenus a celle benoite gloire.   35
    La .xiie. estoille, qui est la principale de leur
gloire, sera la vision de celle Benoite Trinité du Pere, du
Filz, et du Saint Esperit en unité d'essence divine ou
ilz se mireront et la contempleront incessamment, dont la
joye et delectation est a nous incomprenable et non mie a   40
eulx saoulable, si comme sont a nous noz communs plasirs et
joyes, mais plus delictable de tant comme plus est regardee;
verront de leurs yeulx corporelz ce throne imperial et
magesté glorieuse avironnee de cherubins et seraphins,
rendans voix de merveilleuse melodie, beneissant et louant   45
Dieu continuelment, remirant le bel ordre par degrez ou sont
assises les creatures glorieuses, la estans chascune selon

and consolation that they will feel in the perfect peace,
love, and union that will be among them, or that they will
have with Jesus Christ; they will love God perfectly for the
sake of His goodness, the others for the love of God, all
in one will and concord, as one body, one triumphant Church,   5
God's spouse around whom they will be as His people, although
one may be more elevated than the other by his merits, but
all will have them largely, sufficiently, and without envy;
they will see their king Jesus Christ on His throne, who
will love them, as He says in His gospel that He is the good   10
shepherd who knows His flock, and for whom He died in order
to take them away from their enemy.

The tenth star is the incomprehensible joy that they
will feel when seeing themselves so loved and cherished by
their Creator, God the Father, who will treat them as the   15
sons of Jesus Christ, and who will call them brothers, and
give them so many great gifts and perfect graces; they will
talk together of them and rejoice, recognizing Him as their
Father who will have made them the heirs of His blessed
Kingdom and His infinite glory. The eleventh will be the   20
perfect happiness and great pleasure that they will take--
perfectly, indeed with all their might--in this Holy
Trinity which is one God, and they will be so united to Him
with glowing affection for His infinite goodness, that they
will burn with loving affection, with the thought of all   25
the good things that they have received from Him, that they
will be all quenched, and almost drunk by this pleasure,
thinking how God the Father deigned to send His Son, God
the Son, the second person of the Trinity, to earth to take
on human flesh for them, to be embodied in the Virgin Mary,   30
and to take a human body, the blessed Jesus Christ, who
suffered such a bitter death to redeem the pains into which
they had fallen through the sin of the first parents; and
how God the Holy Spirit will have enlightened them so much
that they are repentant, and their sins redeemed, and   35
through whom they will come to this blessed glory.

The twelfth star, which is the foremost of their glory,
will be the vision of this blessed Trinity of the Father,
the Son, and the Holy Spirit in the unity of divine essence,
and in which they will see themselves and contemplate   40
incessantly, and whose joy and delight are not comprehensible
to us, but for which they are unsatiable, just as our common
pleasures and joys are to us, but the more it is beheld,
the more pleasure it gives; they will see with their corporeal eyes this imperial throne and glorious majesty,   45
surrounded by cherubim and seraphim, voicing marvelous
melodies, blessing and praising God incessantly, admiring

son merite, tous contens et assouvis, sans plus querir vouloir, ne desirer, habondans en toute joye permanablement, habitans en celle très sainte court celeste, de la quelle, a bon droit, dist Saint Augustin: "O, com glorieuses choses sont dittes de toy, benoite cité de Dieu!" Dont disoit Saint Gregoire, que il nul n'est qui comprendre peust la grandeur des choses qui y sont, ne entendement le concevoir--comme estre tousjours assistant de nostre Conditeur--veoir le visage de Dieu, la Benoite Trinité face a face, regarder a lumiere incomprehensible, estre tousjours present la compaignie des anges avec les benois esperis, n'avoir jamais paour de la mort, et soy esjoïr ou don de perpetuité. Et pour ce, ces choses contemplant, disoit Saint Bernart: "O, gloire eternele, joye incomprenable, vision de paix, souffisance acomplie, compaignie beneuree, felicité celeste, asseuré repos, infalible bien, tant sont eureux ceulx qui la se treuvent, au quel bien et gloire nous permaint enfin le Pere et le Filz et le Saint Esperit, un seul Dieu, Amen!"

La fin et conclusion.

A revenir au premier propos et conclure la .v^e. raison que au devant te mis, ma redoubtee Dame, comme je me soie, si me semble, assez souffisamment de promesse acquité de te demoustrer par ce qui est dit la difference d'entre la vie presente et celle que ont les trepassez en grace en l'autre siecle, dont en concluant te dis de rechief, si que pour veoir par les susdittes preuves tu le pues clerement, que achoison n'as de douloir ne de plaindre la mort des susdis tes amis trespassez par grace de Dieu--si comme je tiens finez salutairement--aux quelz pevent plus prouffiter aumosnes, oraisons et bienfais que ne font tes lermes; veu les grans biens dont ilz sont, se Dieu plaist, attendans, qui est la gloire du ciel, a la quelle les parmaint et toy avec enfin ycellui Dieu qui de toutes choses est principe et atteur, qui garde de toy soit!

Escript a Paris par moy, Cristine de Pizan, ton humble et obeissant, suppliant humblement que a mal tu n'aies, ne moins gré ne m'en saches se plus tost n'as de moy eue ceste presente espitre; la quelle ta benignité veuille en gré recevoir, et me soit du default de tant y avoir mis--quoyque dés pieça elle feust pour toy en ma pensee--s'il te plaist, souffisant excusacion pluseurs grans ennuis et troubles de courage qui, a cause de maints desplaisirs qui, depuis le temps que je le commençay qui fut dés pieça, ont mon povre entendement, pour sa foiblece, tenu si empeschié en tristes

the beautiful order in steps where the glorious creatures
are placed, each one according to his merit, all contented
and satisfied, not wanting anything more, not desiring,
with a permanent abundance of joys, residing in this very
holy celestial court, of which Saint Augustine says rightly: 5
"Oh, how glorious are the things said of you, blessed City
of God!" Saint Gregory said that no one can understand
the grandeur of the things there, no mind can imagine--since
it is always dependent on our Creator--to see the face of
God, to be face to face with the Holy Trinity, to see an   10
incomprehensible light, the company of angels being forever
present with the blessed spirits, never to fear death, and
to enjoy forever the gift of immortality. On that subject,
considering these things, Saint Bernard says: "Oh, eternal
glory, incomprehensible joy, vision of peace, complete   15
satisfaction, blessed company, celestial felicity, assured
repose, infallible good, all who are there are happy, to
which good and glory, may the Father and the Son and the
Holy Spirit, one God, allow us to be finally, Amen!"

The end and conclusion.   20

     To return to my first topic, and to draw a conclusion
to the fifth reason that I mentioned to you before, my
Revered Lady, and since I have, so it seems to me, fulfilled
well enough the promise to show to you by what is written
the difference between the present life and the one that   25
those who died in grace have in the other world, thus in
conclusion, I will say again that, if you can see clearly
through the aforementioned proofs, that you do not have
reason to mourn nor to pity the death of your aforementioned
friends--whom I think ended in salvation--but who can   30
profit more from alms, prayers, and good deeds than from
your tears, considering the great goods that they expect,
God willing, and which is the glory of Heaven, where may
they and you remain finally with this God, who is the
principle and author of all things, and may He keep you!   35
     Written in Paris by me, Christine de Pizan, your humble
and obedient servant, who humbly prays that you will not
take it badly, or think less of me if you have not received
this present epistle from me; may Your Kindness receive it
with pleasure, and may a sufficient excuse for the fault of   40
having written too much--although it has been in my mind
for a long time--please consist in the great worries and
troubles of courage which because of many displeasures that,
since the moment I started it, and it was long ago, have
kept my poor understanding in such check with all these   45

ymaginacions et pensees qu'il n'a esté en ma puissance de plus tost l'avoir achevé que a cestui .xxe. jour de janvier, l'an mil CCCCXVII.

sad thoughts and ideas, that it has not been in my power to finish it earlier than this twentieth day of January of the year 1417.

An Epistle to the
Queen of France

Une Epistre a la Royne de France

A trés excellent, redoubtee et puissant princesse, Ma Dame Ysabel, Royne de France.

Trés haulte, puissant et trés redoubtee Dame, vostre
excellent dignité ne veuille avoir en desdaing ne despris la   5
voix plourable de moy, sa povre serve, ainz daingne encliner
a notter les parolles dittes par affeccion desireuse de
toute bonne adresce, non obstant que sembler vous pourroit
qu'a si povre, ignorant et indigne personne n'appartiengne
se chargier de si grans choses. Mais comme ce soit de commun 10
ordre que toute personne souffrant aucun mal naturellement
affine au remede, si comme nous veons les malades pourchacier
garrison et les familleux courir a la viande, et ainsi toute
chose a son remede.
Trés redoubtee Dame, ne vous soit doncques merveille se   15
a vous--qui, au dit et oppinion de tous, povez estre la
medecine et souverain remede de la garison de ce royaume a
present playé et navré piteusement, et en peril de piz--ore
se trait et tourne, non mie vous supplier pour terre

No heading BCD   *Before text*: Ensuit une epistre que
Christine de Pisan qui fist ce livre envoia a la royne de
France a Meleun, ou avecques elle Monseigneur d'Orleans, qui
la faisoit grand assemblé de gens d'armes a l'encontre des
ducs de Bourgoingne et de Lembourde et du conte de Nevers,
freres qui estoient a Paris, qui pareillement assembloient
gens de toutes pars. Et estoient, que d'un costé, que
d'autres, bien Xm. combatans, pour laquelle cause la bonne
ville de Paris et tout le royaume furent en grant aventure
d'estre destruis a celle fois se Dieu n'y eust remedié, assi
fist-il, car a l'aide des Roys de Scale et de Navarre et de
ducs de Berry et de Bourbon avecques eulx le conseil du Roy,
bone paix y fu trouvee et se departirent les gens d'armes
d'un costé et d'autre, sans nul mal faire a leur partement C
3. par la grace de Dieu *after* Ysabel BCD, Isabelle CD 5. a
not en B,   ou *not* ne D 7. affeccioun D 9. n'appartient
D 10. de *omitted before* commun CD 13. guerisoun *passim* D
18. on *not* ore BCD

An Epistle to the Queen of France

To the Excellent, Revered and Powerful Princess, My Lady Isabella, Queen of France

Most High, Powerful and Revered Lady, may your Excellent
Dignity not disdain or despise this tearful voice of mine,   5
your humble servant, but rather deign to note the words
dictated by an affection desirous of instructing well,
although it might appear to you that it is not the business
of such a poor, ignorant and unworthy person to engage in
such important matters. But just as it is a natural thing   10
for anyone who suffers from an illness to find a remedy, so
can we see the sick look for recovery and the hungry run for
food, and thus all things seek a remedy.
Most Revered Lady, do not therefore wonder if to you--
who, according to everyone's opinions and beliefs, can be   15
the medicine and sovereign remedy for this kingdom now so
pitifully wounded and injured, and in danger of worse--I turn
and come, not to beg you on behalf of a foreign land, but on
behalf of your own land and natural heritage of your very

estrange, mais pour vostre propre lieu et naturel heritaige
a voz trés nobles enfans. Trés haute Dame et ma trés
redoubtee, non obstant que vostre sens soit tout adverti et
advisié de ce qu'il appartient, touteffoiz est-il vray que
vous, seant en vostre trosne royal couronné de honneurs, ne   5
povez savoir, fors par autruy rappors, les communes
besoingnes, tant en parolles comme en faiz, qui queurent
entre les subjiez.

Pour ce, haulte Dame, ne vous soit grief oïr les ramen-
tevances en piteux regrais des adouléz supplians Françoys,   10
a present reampliz d'affliccion et tretresse, qui a humble
voix plaine de plours crient a vous, leur souveraine et
redoubtee Dame, priant, pour Dieu mercy, que humble pitié
vueille monstrer a vostre begnin cuer leur desolacion et
misere, pay cy que prouchaine paix entre ces .II. haulz   15
princes germains de sanc et naturelment amis, mais a present
par estrange Fortune meuz a aucune contencion, ensemble
veuilliez procurer et empetrer.

Et chose est assez humaine et commune mesmement: sou-
ventefoiz vient entre pere et fils aucun descort. Mais   20
dyabolique est et seroit la perseverance en la quelle povez
notter par especial deux grans et horribles maulx et dommages. L'un que il convendroit en brief temps que le
royame en feust destruit, si, comme dit Notre Seigneur en
l'Euvangile: "Le royame en soy divisié sera desolé."   25
L'autre que hayne perpetuelle soit nee et nourrie d'orez en
avant entre les hoirs et enfans du noble sang de France, les
quels seulent estre un propre corps et pillier a la deffense
de cestui dit royame, pour la quelle cause d'ancien nom est
appellee fort et puissant.   30

Trés excellent et redoubtee Dame, encores vous plaise
notter et reduire a memoire trois trés grans biens et
prouffiz qui par ceste paix procurer vous ensuivroient. Le
premier appartient a l'ame, a la quelle trés souverain

1. propre *omitted* D   2. dame *omitted* B, dame *after*
redoubtee D   3. bon *before* sens BD   5. majesté *not* trosne
D   7. cuerent B, courrent D   8. vos *not* les BCD, subjiez
passim D   9. de *before* oïr D   11. tristess BCD   15.
proschainement D   16. monsire le duc d'Orlie[ns et] celluy
de Bourgong[ne] *in marginal note* B   17. aucune *omitted* B,
contencioun D, vie et C   22. trés *not* grans B   24. si
comme Nostre Seignur dit D   25. divisié en soy B
26. serroit *not* soit BCD   28. souloient CD, comme un BCD
28. defance de cestuy royaume CD   29. ancien *omitted* B, nom
omitted D   32. a noter C   34. primer, alme D, acquerrez
trés souverain merite BCD

noble children. Most High and Revered Lady, although your
mind is well aware and told of what it should know, it may
nevertheless be true that you, seated on your royal throne
surrounded with honors, cannot know, except by someone's
report, the common problems, in words as well as in facts,   5
which prevail upon your subjects.

For this reason, High Lady, do willingly hear the
complaints and pitiful regrets of the suffering and suppliant
French people now full of affliction and sadness, and who
cry with tearful voices to you, their supreme and revered   10
Lady, praying, by the mercy of God, that a humble pity may
show to your tender heart their desolation and misery, so
that you can procure and obtain peace soon between these
two princes of the same blood and who are loved ones by
nature, but who are at present brought to a quarrel by   15
strange Fortune.

This is a very human and common occurrence: there is
often disagreement between father and son. But the continu-
ation of it is and would be the work of the devil, especially
when you take note of its two great and horrible evils   20
and injuries. One is that the kingdom would be destroyed
by it in a short time if, as says Our Lord in the Gospel:
"The kingdom divided within itself will be destroyed."[1] The
other is that a perpetual hatred would spring up and remain
henceforth between the heirs and children of the noble   25
blood of France, they who are wont to be one united body
and the pillar that defends this kingdom, which is called
strong and powerful by virtue of a very old name.

My Excellent and Revered Lady, do still note and
remember three great goods and benefits which would ensue   30
after you had secured peace. The first belongs to the soul,
whose very sovereign merit you would acquire by the fact
that, thanks to you, a great and shameful effusion of blood
in the very Christian kingdom of France established by God

[1]*Luke* 2.7.

merite acquerriez, de ce que par vous seroit eschevee si
grant et si honteuse effusion de sang ou trés chrestien et de
Dieu establi royaume de France, et la confusion qui en
ensuivroit, se tel horreur avoit duree. Item le IIe bien,
que vous seriez pourchaceresse de paix et cause de la resti-   5
tucion du bien de vostre noble porteure et de leurs loyaulx
subgiez. Le tiers bien, qui ne fait a desprisier, c'est
qu'en perpetuelle memoire de vous, ramenteue, recommandee et
louee es croniques et nobles gestes de France, doublement
couronnee de honneur seriez, avec l'amour, graces, presens et   10
humbles grans merciz de voz loyaulz subgiez.

Et ma redoubtee Dame, a regarder aux raisons de vostre
droit, posons qu'il soit ou feust ainsi que la dignité de
vostre haultesse se tenist de l'une des partiez avoir aucunement blecee, par quoy vostre hault cuer feust mains evolu que 15
par ceste paix feust traictiee. O trés noble Dame, quel
grant scens c'est aucunefoiz, mesmes entre les plus grans,
laissier aler partie de son droit pour eschiver plus grant
inconvenient ou attaindre a trés grant bien et utilité! Et,
trés puissant Dame, les histoires de vos devanciers qui   20
deuement se gouvernerent, ne vous doivent estre exemple de
bien vivre, si comme il advent jadis a Romme d'une trés puissant princesse de la quelle le filz par les barons de la cité
avoit esté a grant tort et sans cause bannis et chaciez; dont
aprés, pour celle injure vengier, comme il eust assemblé si   25
grant ost que souffisant estoit pour tout destruire, la vaillant dame, non obstant le villenie faite, ne vint-elle au
devant de son filz, et tant fist qu'elle appaisa son yre et
le pacifia aux Rommains?

Helas! Honnouree Dame, doncques quant il avendra que   30
pitié, charitié, clemence et benignité ne sera trouvee en

1. serroit par vous B, grant grif du peuple cristien D
3. le *before* royaume CD   4. tielle erreur CD   4. deusiesme
B, second D   5. porteresse BCD, restauration BC, restaura-
cioun D   7. iiie D, qui ne *omitted* D   8. los *not* vous BCD
10. avecques D, couronee seriez C   11. merites *not* mercis C
12. trés *before* redoubtee D   13. fust ou soit D, ainsi
omitted D   14. a *not* de C, avoir esté BC   15. moins BCD, a
ce *before* que D, vous *before* que BCD   16. traitee CD, Hé
not O B, doulce *not* noble C, quant *not* quel C   19. soun, pur
D, mal et *before* inconvenient B, pour *before* atteindre BCD,
plus *not* trés B, Hee *not* Et BCD   20. nos *not* vos BCD,
devanters D   21. gouvernoient CD, nous *not* vous BCD
doivent-elles BCD   22. Rome CD   24. grant *omitted* C, senz
not sans D   25 icelle D   28. apoisa D   29. Romains D
30. il en avra D

could be avoided by your efforts, and so would the confusion
which would follow if such a horror were to last. Similarly,
by the second good, you would be the seeker of peace and the
cause for the restitution of the goods of your noble children
and their loyal subjects. The third good, which is not to   5
be despised, is that in eternal remembrance of you, you would
be remembered, commanded, and praised in the chronicles and
noble tales of France, twice crowned with honors, with love,
presents, graces and humble and deep gratitude from your
loyal subjects.   10

    My Revered Lady, looking at the reasons for the justice
of your position, let us assume that it may be or may have
been the case that Your Highness' dignity has been injured
by one of the parties, and therefore your noble heart is
less disposed to have peace be obtained. Oh, Most Noble   15
Lady, what great mind, even among the greatest, has not
sometimes relinquished its right in order to avoid a greater
disaster or obtain a very great good and usefulness? Most
Powerful Lady, should the tales of your predecessors who
reigned nobly not be an example of good behavior to you,   20
just as it once happened in Rome to a very powerful princess
whose son had been banished and exiled very unfairly and
without cause by the barons of the city; and after that,
since he had, in order to avenge this injury, assembled an
army so large that it was enough to destroy all, did the   25
valiant lady, in spite of the villainy done, not face her
son, and did no much that she pacified his anger, and made
him make peace with the Romans?[2]

    Alas, Honored Lady, if it happens that pity, charity,
clemency and love can not be found in a high princess, where   30
then shall it be found? For since these virtues are by

[2]Veturia prayed to Fortuna to persuade her son
Coriolanus to raise the siege of Rome (Livy 2.40) in 491 B.C.
Also in *Cité des dames* (Richards II.34.1).

haute princesse, ou sera elle doncques quise? Car comme
naturelment en femenines condicions soient les dictes vertus,
plus par rayson doivent habonder et estre en noble dame, de
tant comme elle reçoit plus de dons de Dieu. Et encores a ce
propos qu'il appartient a haute princesse et dame estre   5
moyennerresse de traictié de paix, il appert par les vaillans
dames louees es Saintes Escriptures: si comme la vaillant
saige royne Hester, qui par son sens et benignité appaisa
l'yre du roy Assuaire, tant que revocquer fist la sentence
donnee contre le pueple condampné a mort. Aussi Bersabee   10
n'appaisa elle maintes foiz l'yre David? Aussi une vaillant
royne qui consseilla a son mari que puis qu'il ne povoit
avoir par force ses ennemis, que il feist si comme font les
bons medecins: les quelx quant ils voyent que medecines
ameres ne prouffictent a leurs paciens, ils leur donnent des   15
doulces. Et par celle voye, le fist la saige royne recon-
cilier a ses adversaires.

 Semblablement se pourroient dire infiniz exemples que
je laisse pour briefté des saiges roynes louees, et par le
contraire des perverses, crueuses et ennemies de nature   20
humaine: si comme la faulse royne Jezabel et autres semblables, qui, pour leurs demerites sont encores et perpetuelle-
ment seront diffamees, maudites et dampnees. Mais des
bonnes, encore a nostre propos sanz plus loing querir, la
trés saige et bonne royne de France, Blanche, mere de Saint   25
Louys, quant les barons estoient en descort pour cause de
regenter le royame, ne prenoit-elle son filz mendre d'aage
entre ses bras, et entre les barons le tenoit disant: "Ne
voyez-vous vostre roy? Ne faites chose dont, quant Dieu
l'ara conduit en aage de discretion, il se doye d'aucun de   30
vous tenir pour mal content." Et ainsi par son sens les
appaisoit.

 2. naturelment *omitted* D, condiciouns D 3. plus
omitted D, estre *after* doivent D, de tant qu'elle D
4. cest propost D 5. appartiegne D 7. Escriptures louees
B 10. peuple *passim* D, auxi D, Barsabee D, n'apois D
11. ire de David BCD, auxi D, une autre BCD 12. puis q'il
fist D 15. profitent D 20. de perverses D 21. de la B,
Gyesabel D 24. senz querir plus loing CD 25. et *omitted*
before bonne BCD, mere Seint BCD, ses *not* les CD 26. a
not en CD 27. le royame *omitted* CD, la royne ne prenoit CD,
d'ans CD 28. elle le tenoit CD 29. veez *not* voyez D
30. avra D, aege D, discrecioun D, doy tenir mal content
d'aucun de vous CD, pour *omitted* B

nature in the female sex, they must reasonably be the more abundant in a noble lady, the more so since she receives more gifts from God. And still on the subject that it behooves a high princess and lady to be the mediator of a peace treaty, it is shown in the worthy ladies praised in the   5
Holy Scriptures: thus, the worthy and wise Queen Esther, who appeased the anger of King Ahasuerus by her common sense and goodness, so much so that she had the sentence against the people condemned to death revoked.[3] Did Bathsheba not appease David's anger many times as well? Also a worthy   10
queen who advised her husband that since he could not vanquish his enemies by force, he should do what the good physicians do: that is when they see that bitter medicines do not help their patients, they give them sweet ones. And in this way, the wise queen caused him to become reconciled   15
with his adversaries.

    Similarly, could infinite examples of wise and praise-worthy queens be given, but I will leave them for the sake of brevity; the same could be done with opposite examples of perverse and cruel queens, enemies of humankind: thus, the   20
false queen Jezebel and others of the same kind, who because of their evil actions are still and will be forever infamous, accursed, and damned. But of the good queens, for our purpose and in order not to search further, [there is] the very wise and good Queen of France, Blanche, mother of Saint   25
Louis.[4] When the barons quarreled over the regency of the kingdom, did she not take her child, still very young, in her arms, and holding him among the barons, say: "Do you not see your king? Do not do anything that, when God has guided him to the age of reason, he will blame on any one of you."   30
And so she appeased them with her good advice.

[3]Esther is also in *Cité des dames* (Richards, II.32.1).
[4]Blanche of Castille in *Cité des dames* (Richards, I.13.2).

Trés haute Dame, mais que mon langaige ne vous tourne
a ennuy, encores vous dis-je que, tout ainsi comme la Royne
du ciel, mere de Dieu, est appellee mere de toute chris-
tienté, doit estre dicte et appellee toute saige et bonne
royne, mere et conffortarresse, et advocate de ses subjiez   5
et de son pueple. Helas, doncques, qui seroit si dure mere
qui peust souffrir, se elle n'avoit le cuer de pierre, veoir
ses enfans entre-occire, et espendre le sang l'un a l'autre,
et leurs povres membres destruire et disperser, et puist,
qu'il venist par de costé aucuns estrangiers, qui du tout   10
les persecutassent et saisissent leurs heritaiges?
    Et ainsi, trés haute Dame, povez estre certaine conven-
droit qu'avenist ainsi de ceste persecution, se la chose
aloit plus avant, que Dieux ne vueille! Car n'est mie doubte
que les ennemis du royame, resjouiz de ceste aventure, ven-   15
droient par de costé a grant armée pour tout parhonnir. Ha,
Dieu! Quel douleur a si noble royaume perdre et perir tel
chevalerie! Helas! Et qu'il convenist que le povre pueple
comparast le pechié dont il est innocent! Et que les
povres petits alaittans et enfans criassent aprés leurs   20
lasses meres veufves et adolues, mourans de faim, et elles,
desnuees de leurs biens, n'eussent de quoy les appaisier!
Les quelles voix, comme racontent en plusieurs lieux les
Escriptures, percent les cieulz par pitié devant Dieu juste
et attrayent vengence sur ceulx qui en sont cause.   25
    Et encores avec ce, quel honte a ce royaume qu'il
convenist que les pouvres, desers de leurs biens, alassent
mendier par famine en estranges contrees en racomptant
comment ceulx qui garder les devoient les eussent destruits!
Dieux! Comment seroit jamais si lait diffame, non accoustumé 30
en ce noble royaume repparé ne remis? Et certes, noble Dame,

2. tourt D, dige D, aussi CD   3. diel *not* du D, mere
omitted before de toute CD, cristianté D   4. dit D
5. mere conforteresse CD, et advocate *omitted* D   6. royne
crossed out before mere   7. souffrir *omitted* CD, cueur D
9. puist D   10. aucuns *omitted* BCD, estranges annemies B,
estranges ennemys CD   11. laissassent *not* saisissent CD
12. estre toute CD   13. en fin *not* ainsi BCD   15. roialme B
16. o *not* a CD   18. et *omitted* CD   20. pouveres D, alleic-
tans D   21. adolees B, adoulees CD   23. quant a Dieu
before comme racontent CD, quant ce advient B   24. Escriptures *after* lieux BC, perçant B, percient CD, cielx D, par
pitié *omitted* B   28. en racontent CD *and before* contrees CD
29. come CD   30. ce *not* si D, se B   31. noble *added in
between lines*, trés noble CD

Epistle to the Queen

Most High Lady, although I hope that my words do not
annoy you, I will also tell you that, just as the Queen of
Heaven, Mother of God, is called mother of all Christendom,
so must be said and called any wise and good queen, mother
and comforter, advocate of her subjects and her people.   5
Alas! Who could be such a harsh mother to be able to endure,
if she did not have a heart of stone, to see her children
kill one another, and spill each other's blood, and cut and
scatter each other's limbs and then see foreigners come
along who would pursue them to the end and seize their   10
inheritance?

Therefore, Most High Lady, you can be sure that such
disaster would necessarily happen in this way, if the thing
continued, and may God not will it! Because there is no
doubt that the enemies of the kingdom, rejoicing at this turn   15
of events, would come along with a great army to dishonor
all. Oh, God! What pain would it be to such a noble kingdom to lose and see perish such knights! Alas! That the
poor people should have to pay for the sin of which they
are innocent! That the poor little infants and children   20
should cry for their miserable and suffering widowed mothers,
in a state of starvation, and their mothers, deprived of all
their goods, should not have anything to appease them!
Their pitiful voices, as the Holy Scriptures tell in several
passages, pierce the heavens before God who is just, and   25
ask for vengeance on those who are the cause of it.

And furthermore, what shame would it be to this kingdom
that the poor people, deprived of their possessions, should
beg, because of the famine, in foreign lands telling how
those who had to protect them ruined them! God! How would   30
such an ugly infamy, unusual in this noble kingdom, ever be

nous veons a present les apprestes de ces mortelz inconveniens, qui ja sont si avanciez que très maintenant en y
a de destruitz et desers de leurs biens, et detruit-on tous
les jours de piz en piz, tant que qui est crestien en doit
avoir pitié. Et oultre ce, seroit encore a notter a cellui   5
prince ou princesse qui le cuer aroit tant obstiné en pechié,
qu'il n'accompteroit nulle chose a Dieu ne a si fortes
douleurs, s'il n'estoit du tout fol ou folle, les trés
variables tours de Fortune, qui, en un tout seul moment, se
puet changier et muer.   10
    Dieux! A quans coups eust pensé la royne Olimpias,
mere du grant Alexandre, ou temps qu'elle veoit tout le monde
soulz ses piez, a elle subgiet et obeissant, que Fortune eust
puissance de la conduire ou point ou quel piteusement fina
ses jours a grant honte? Et semblablement d'assés d'autres   15
pourroit-on dire. Mais qu'en advient-il, quant Fortune a
ainsi acqueilly aucun puissant? Se si saigement n'a tant
fait le temps passé, par le moyen d'amours, de pitié et
charité qu'il ait acquiz Dieu premierement et bien vueillans
au monde, toute sa vie et ses faiz sont racontez en publique   20
et tournez en repprouche. Et tout ainsi comme a un chien
qui est chacié tous lui queurent sus, et est celli de tous
deffoulez, en criant sus lui qu'il est bien employez.
    Trés excellant et ma trés redoubtee Dame, infinies
raisons vous pourroient estre reccordees des causes qui vous   25
doivent mouvoir a pitié et a traictié de paix, les quelles
vostre bon scens n'ignore mie. Si fineray a tant mon
espitre, suppliant vostre digne majesté qu'elle l'ait
agreable et soit favourable a la plourable requeste par moy
escripte de vos povres sujiez, loyaulz Françoys. Et tout   30
ainsi comme c'est plus grant charité de donner au povre une

1. jugemens *not* inconveniens CD   3. en detruit CD
4. a cause de la grant foyzon de gens d'armes d'un costé et
d'autre B, et *omitted* BCD, qui *omitted* CD   5. oultre et BCD
6. aroit *after* obstiné B, en pechié *omitted* BCD   7. toutes
si saintes douleurs BCD   8. tout *omitted* BCD   10. puent
changer CD   11. Diex D, a *omitted* CD, cops C   12. Alixandre D   13. subgiet et *omitted* B   14. au *not* ou CD, quelle
D   16. avient quant CD   17. acuilli D, puissant seigneur
ou dame CD   18. pitié *before* amours B, de *omitted* CD, ou
not et CD   19. eit *not* ait D, primerement D, premier B,
vellans amys D   20. conptés BCD   21. tous *not* tournez CD
22. chassiez D, seure *not* sus BCD, et *omitted* B, celui D
23. defoulés D, sur BCD   25. dictes *not* recordees B
27. sen CD   28. a vostre CD   30. loiaulx D   31. aussi CD,
c['est] *omitted* CD

rectified or forgotten? Indeed, noble lady, we can see now
the preparations for these disasters, which are so well under
way that there are at present many people ruined and deprived
of their possessions, and every day worse and worse is done,
so much so that whoever is a Christian must feel pity.   5
Moreover, a prince or princess who would be so obstinate in
sin that he/she would render no account to God or to such
great sufferings, should be reminded, if he/she were not
completely mad, of the very variable turns of Fortune, which
can change and transform itself at any time.   10
    God! Did Queen Olympias, mother of the great Alexander,
think, when she had everyone under her feet, subjected and
obedient to her, of the many blows that Fortune would have
the power to inflict on her and to the point where she
piteously and shamefully ended her days?[5] And we could tell 15
similar stories of many other people. What happens to the
powerful man thus welcomed by Fortune? If he did not act
wisely in the past, and by the means of love, pity, and
charity had not first attracted God and not done well in
this world, then his whole life and actions are told in   20
public and put to shame. And as a dog is pursued by all who
are chasing it away, this man is trampled by all, and they
all shout at him that he is being deservedly treated.
    My Excellent and Most Revered Lady, you could be told
infinite reasons for the causes which must move you to   25
pity and to negotiate peace, and your good sense does know
them. Thus I will finish my epistle, begging your worthy
majesty that she receive it well and that she be favorable
to the teary request of mine written on behalf of your poor
subjects, the loyal French people. And just as it is a   30
deed of greater charity to give a bit of bread to the poor in

[5]Olympias seized power after the death of Alexander in
317 B.C., but was put to death herself in Pydna the following
year.

piece de pain en temps de chierté et de famine, que ung tout
entier en temps de fertilité et d'abondance, a vostre povre
pueple vueillez donner en temps de tribulacion une piecete
de la parolle et du labour de vostre hautesse et puissance,
sera, s'il vous plaist, assez souffisant pour les rassadier   5
et garir du desir familleux qu'ilz ont de paix. Et ils
prieront Dieu pour vous; pour le quel bien accomplir et
mains autres, Dieu par sa grace vous vueille conceder et
ottroier bonne vie et longue, et a la fin, gloire pardurable.
Escript le ve jour d'octombre, l'an de grace mil .IIII. c.   10
et cinq.

Vostre trés humble obeissant
creature,

Christine de Pizan

Prenez en gré, s'il vous plaist, cest escript   15
De ma main fait aprés mie nuit une heure.

Noble seigneur, pour qui je l'ay escript
Prenez en gré.

Quant vous plaira mieulz vous sera rescript
Mais n'avoye nul autre clerc a l'eure.   20

Prenez en gré, s'il v ...

1. cherté D   2. fertilitee D   3. veullez CD, ce temps
CD, de fertilité *crossed out before* tribulacion, un piece CD
5. la quelle comme ils tiennent serra BCD, s'il vous plaist
omitted CD, rassasier BCD   6. guerier D   10. octobre BCD,
de grace *omitted* CD, CCCC et cinque BCD   12. et trés
obeissante CD   14. Puzan CD   15. *rondeau missing* BCD

the time of high prices and famine, than a whole loaf in the
time of fertility and abundance, do give to your people in a
time of tribulation a small portion of the words and efforts
of your highness and power, which, if you please, would be
enough to sate them and to cure them of the hungry desire   5
for peace that they have. And they will pray for you; and
for this good action and many others, may God by His Grace
give and grant you a good and long life, and at the end,
perpetual glory. Written the 5th day of October, the year
of grace 1405.   10

                        Your very humble and obedient
                        subject

                        Christine de Pizan

    Take in good part, if you please, this writing done
    By my hand after one hour after midnight.   15

    Noble Lord, for whom I wrote it
    Take it in good part.

    Whenever you want, it will be better rewritten for you
    But I did not have any other clerk at the moment.

    Take it in good part, if you ...   20

    [6]According to *Pinet* (p. 131), the "noble seigneur" in
the rondeau had to be the duke of Orléans who was to give
the epistle to the queen.

Lament on the Evils
of the Civil War

Lamentacion sur les maux de la guerre civile

Qui a point de pitié la mette en oevre,
Veez-cy le temps qui le requiert.

Seulette a part, et estraignant a grant paine les
lermes qui ma veue troublent et comme fontaine affluent sur   5
mon visage, tant que avoir puisse espace de escripre ceste
lasse complainte, dont la pitié de l'eminent meschief me
fait d'ameres goutes effacier l'escripture, je m'esbahiz et
en complaignant dis: O! Comment puet-ce estre que cuer
humain, tant soit la Fortune estrange, si puist ramener   10
homme a nature de trés devorable et cruele beste? Ou est
doncques la raison qui li donne le non de animal raisonnable? Comment est-il en la puissance de Fortune de
telement transmuer homme, que convertiz soit en serpent,
ennemi de nature humaine? O las! Veez-cy de quoy, nobles   15
princes françois! Et ne vous desplaise, ou est a present
le doulz sang naturel d'entre vous, lequel desonques seult
estre le droit comble de la benignité du monde? De quoy
trés les temps anciens sont raemplies toutes autentiques
histoires, et de qui Fama seult corner ses chançons par tout   20
l'universel monde. Que sont devenuz les clers yeulx du
noble entendement, qui, par nature et longue coustume, vous
faisoient ouvrer par conseil de preudes hommes de juste
conscience? Sont-ilz or aveuglez, comme il semble, vos
peres de la congregacion francoise, soubz les quelz ayolz   25
seullent estre gardez, deffenduz et nourriz les multitudes
des enfans de la terre jadiz beneuree, ore convertie en
desolacion, se pitié n'y labeure? Que vous ont meffait
ceulx qui comme Dieu vous aourent, et qui en toutes terres
pour honneur de vous se renomment? Les quelx semble que a   30
present vueilliez traittier, non pas comme filz, maiz
ennemis mortelz, par ce que les discors d'entre vous leur
pourchassent, c'est assavoir: grief, guerre, et bataille.
    Pour Dieu! Pour Dieu! Princes trés haulx, ouvrez les
yeulx par tel savoir, que ja vous semble veoir comme chose   35

Lament on the Evils of the Civil War

Whoever has pity, let him put it to use
The time which requires it has come.

Alone, and suppressing with great difficulty the tears
which blur my sight and pour down my face like a fountain,   5
so much that I am surprised to have the time to write this
weary lament, whose writing the pity for the coming disaster
makes me erase with bitter tears, and I say in pain: Oh,
how can it be that the human heart, as strange as Fortune
is, can make man revert to the nature of a voracious and   10
cruel beast? Where is reason which gives him the name of
rational animal? How can Fortune have the power to
transform man so much, that he is changed into a serpent,
the enemy of humankind? Oh, alas, here is the reason why,
noble French princes. With deference to you, where is now   15
the sweet natural blood among you which has been for a long
time the true summit of kindness in the world? The ancient
times are full of all true stories about it, and Fame used
to sing its praise throughout the whole world. What became
of the sharp eyes of understanding which wise men of just   20
conscience in their counsel made you open by nature and long
habit? Are the fathers of your French assembly now blind,
as it seems, under whose eyes the numerous children of a
land once blessed, were protected, defended and nurtured, a
land now desolate, if pity does not work its influence?   25
What wrong have those men done to you, they who, like God,
loved you, and who are reputed to honor you in every land?
It seems that you want to treat them, not as sons, but as
mortal enemies, because the discords between you are
haunting them, and these are: grief, war, and battle.   30
For God's sake! For God's sake! High Princes, let
these facts open your eyes and may you see as already accomplished what the preparations for taking arms will do in the
end; thus you will see ruined cities, towns and castles
destroyed, and fortresses razed to the ground. And where?   35

advenue, ce que les apprestes de voz armes prises pourront
conclurre, sy y appercevrez ruynes de citez, destruccions
de villes et chasteaulx, forteresses ruees par terre. Et
en quel part? Ou droit nombril de France! La noble cheva-
lerie et jouvente françoise toute d'une nature, qui, comme   5
un droit ame et corps, seult estre a la deffense de la
couronne et la chose publique, ore assemblee en honteuse
bataille l'un contre l'autre, pere contre filz, frere contre
frere, parens contre autres, a glaives mortelz, couvrans de
sang, de corps mors et de membres les trés doulereux champs.   10
O, la trés dehonnoree victoire a qui que elle remaigne! Quel
gloire li donra Renommee? Sera elle donc de lorier couronnee? Hé! Lasse my, maiz devra estre de trés noires espines
honteusement bendee, soy voiant non pas vainquerresse, mais
homicide de son mesmes sang, dont noirs habiz porter lui   15
appartient comme a mort de parent.

 O tu, chevalier, qui viens de tele bataille, dy-moy, je
t'en prie, quel honneur tu emportes? Diront donc tes gestes
pour toy plus honnorer, que tu feuz a la journee du costé
vainqueur? Mais cestui peril, quoy que en eschappes, soit   20
mis en mescompte de tes autres beaux faiz! Car a journee
reprouchee n'appartient louenge. Hé! Que pleust aux hommes,
car a Dieu bien plairoit, que nul de soy armer n'eust courage ne d'un costé ne d'autre!

 Et que en ensuira aprés, en nom Dieu? Famine, pour la   25
cause du dicipement et gast des biens qui y sera fait, et la
faulte de cultiver les terres, de quoy sourdront rebellions
de peuples par estre des gens d'armes estrangiez et privez,
trop oppressez, mengiez et pilliez de ça et de la; sub-
version es citez par oultrageuse charge, ou, par necessitez   30
de finances avoir, convendra imposer les cytoiens et habi-
tans; et ensurquetout les Angloiz par de costé qui parfe-
ront l'eschec et mat, se Fortune y consent; et encore reste
les discencions et morteles haynes dont traysons sourdront,
qui en infiniz cuers a ceste cause seront enracinees.   35

 Est-il ainsi delibere? Certes oyl! Plourez doncques,
plourez, batant les paulmes a grans criz--si que fist en cas
pareil jadiz la dolente Argine avec les dames d'Arges--dames,
damoiselles et femmes du royaume de France! Car ja sont
aguisiez les glaives qui vous rendront veufves et desnuees   40
d'enfans et de parens! O, dames de la cite de Sabine,

In the very heart of France! The noble knights and youth
of France, all of one nature, one single soul and body,
which used to defend the crown and the public good, are
now gathered in a shameful battle one against another,
father against son, brother against brother, relatives   5
against one another, with deadly swords, covering the pitiful
fields with blood, dead bodies, and limbs. Oh,
dishonorable victory may be to the one who has it! What
glory will Fame give to it? Will it be crowned with laurels?
Ah me, it will have to be shamefully bound with back thorns   10
when it sees itself, not as a victor, but as the very killer
of its own blood, for whom it is appropriate to wear black,
as in the death of kin.

      Oh, you, knight who comes from such a battle, tell me,
I pray you, what honor did you win there? Will they tell   15
of your deeds to honor you more, that you were on the
winning side that day? But may this peril, although you
escaped it, be counted against your other good deeds!
Because it is not proper to praise an adventure which is not
blameless. Oh, would that men, since it would indeed please 20
God, had not, on either side, the courage to bear arms!

      And what will follow, in God's name? Famine, because
of the wasting and ruining of things that will ensue, and
the lack of cultivation, from which will spring revolts by
the people who have been too often robbed, deprived and   25
oppressed, their food taken away and stolen here and there
by soldiers, subversion in the towns because of outrageous
taxes which will have to be levied on the citizens and
dwellers to raise the needed money, and above all, the
English will obtain checkmate on the side, if Fortune agrees   30
to it; and there will also be dissensions and mortal hatreds
which will be rooted in many hearts for this reason and
which will engender treason.

      Is it thus decided? Yes, indeed! So, cry, cry, beat
your hands and cry--as once the sad Argia did in such a   35
case, along with the ladies of Argos--you ladies, damsels,
and women of the kingdom of France![1] Because the swords
that will make you widows and deprive you of your children
and kin have already been sharpened! Oh, Ladies of the city
of the Sabines, we would have needed you for this task, for   40
the dangers and the quarrels that once were between your kin

[1]Argia was the widow of Polynices, son of Oedipus, who
was killed by his brother Eteocles. She went against
Creon's orders that Polynices' corpse not be buried. Also
in *Cité des dames* (Richards II.17.1), where Christine
acknowledges Boccaccio's *De mulieribus claris* for this story.

besoing eussions de vous en ceste besoigne, car n'estoit pas
greigneur le peril et contens jadiz entre vos parens, quant
par grant prudence vous entremeistes de y mettre paix,
lorsque vous fichastes eschevellees, vos petitz enfans entre
braz, ou champ de la bataille, par grans tourbes crians: 5
"Ayez merci de nos chiers amis et parens! Si faites paix!"
    Hé! Royne couronnee de France, dors-tu adés? Et qui
te tient que tantost celle part n'affinz tenir la bride et
arrester ceste mortel emprise? Ne vois-tu en balance l'eritage de tes nobles enfans? Tu, mere des nobles hoirs de   10
France, redoubtee princesse, qui y puet que toy, ne qui
sera-ce, qui a ta seigneurie et auctorité desobeira, se a
droit te veulx de la paix entremettre?
    Venez, venez, vous touz saiges de ce royaume avec
vostre royne! De quoy servez-vous, neiz conseil du roy? Et   15
tous chacun la main y mette. Ja vous souliez vous entremettre neiz des petites choses. De quoy se loera France de
tant de sages testes, se ores ne treuvent voie pour sa
garantise, fontaine de clergie garder a eschever d'estre
perie? Ou sont adés voz entreprises et voz saiges raisons?   20
Hee! Clergie de France, lairas-tu ainsi a Fortune courir
son influence? Pourquoi ne faiz processions par devotes
prieres? Ne vois-tu le besoing? Car ja semble comme Nynyve
que Dieu l'ait a perir condampnee, et que Son yre par les
griefz pechiez qui y habondent l'ait acueillie, dont la   25
chose est en grant doubte, se la sentence n'est revoquee par
intercession de devote oroison.
    Assurez donques, peuples! Devotes femelettes, criez
misericorde pour ceste grief tempeste! Ha! France, France,
jadiz glorieux royaume! Helas, comment diray-je plus? Car   30
trés amers plours et lermes incessables dechieent comme
ruisseaux sur mon papier, si qu'il n'y a place seiche ou
puisse continuer l'escripture de la complainte trés doulou-
reuse, que l'abondance de mon cuer par grant pitié de toy
veult getter hors. Si que assez sont occupees les lasses   35
mains laissent souvent la penne de quoy je escripz, pour
rendre la veue a mes yeulx troublez en torchant les lermes
dont l'abondance me moille piz et giron, quant je pense ce
que diront de toy desoremaiz les Renommees. Car ne seras-tu
pas acomparee de cy en avant aus estranges nacions, la ou   40
les freres germains, cousins et parens par faulse envie et

Lament

were not greater, and you, very wisely, decided to establish
peace when you threw yourselves with hair disheveled into
the battlefield, your children in your arms, and in great
numbers shouted: "Have pity on our dear loved ones! Make
peace!"[2]   5
     Oh, crowned Queen of France, are you still sleeping?
Who prevents you from restraining now this side of your kin
and putting an end to this deadly enterprise? Do you not
see the heritage of your noble children at stake? You, the
mother of the noble heirs of France, Revered Princess, who   10
but you can do anything, and who will disobey your
sovereignty and authority, if you rightly want to mediate
a peace?
     Come, all you wise men of this realm, come with your
queen! What use are you if not for the royal council?   15
Everyone should offer his hand. You used to concern yourselves even with small matters. How shall France be proud
of so many wise men, if now they cannot see to her safety,
and the fount of the clergy keep her from perishing? Where
then are your plans and wise thoughts? Oh, clerics of   20
France, will you let Fortune work its influence? Why do you
not walk in processions and pray devoutly? Do you not feel
the need for it? For you resemble Nineveh, which God
condemned to perish, and which received His wrath because
of the great sins which were many there, and because of this, 25
the situation is very doubtful, unless the sentence is not
revoked by the intercession of devout prayers.[3]
     People, be firm! And you, pious women, cry mercy for
this grievous storm! Ah, France, France, once a glorious
kingdom! Alas, what more can I say? Because bitter and   30
endless tears flow like streams on my paper, there is not
a dry spot where I can pursue the writing of the very painful lament that my heavy heart, for the love of you, wishes
to express. Although they are very busy, my tired hands
often drop the pen with which I write to restore the sight   35
to my eyes, and wipe the many tears which wet my breast and
lap, whenever I think of what Fame will henceforth say of
you. For will you not be compared from now on to the
foreign nations, where brothers, cousins and kin kill each
other like dogs out of false envy and jealousy? Will it not   40
be said with blame: "Go on, go on, you Frenchmen, you who

---

[2]The Sabine women are also mentioned in *Cité des dames*
(Richards II.33.1), and *Mutacion de Fortune* (Solente, v.3,
pp. 183-fol.). [3]In *Jonah 3*, the fall of Nineveh was
averted by penitence. Also in *Mutacion de Fortune* (Solente,
v.1, pp. 152-53).

convoitise s'entre-ocient comme chiens? Ne diront-ils en
reprouchant: "Alez, alez, vous François, qui vous vantiez
du doulz sang de voz princes, non tyrans, et nous eschar-
nissiez de nos usaiges de Guelfes et Guibelins! Or sont-ils
nez en vostre terre. La semence y est germee, que ja n'y   5
fauldra; les païs y sont venuz. Or abaissiez voz cornes, car
vostre gloire est deffaillie.

    Hé, mi! Lasse, trés doulce France! Est-il donques
ainsi qu'en tel peril soies? Certes, oyl. Mais encores y a
il remede. Dieu est misericors. Tout n'est pas mort, quant   10
que gist en peril.

    O! Duc de Berry, noble prince, excellent souche et
estoc des enfans royaulx, filz de roy de France, frere et
oncle, pere d'antiquité de la fleur de liz toute! Comment
est-il possible que ton trés benigne cuer puist souffrir te   15
veoir, a journee precise, en assemblee de bataille mortele
a doulereuses armes contre tes nepveux? Je ne croy pas que
la souvenance de la trés grant amour naturele de leurs peres
et meres, tes trés amez freres et seurs trespassez, souffrist
a nature que lermes et pleurs ne decourussent comme fontaine   20
tout au long de ta face, et que ton noble cuer ne feust de
pitié si comme touz fonduz qu'a paines te soustendroies.
Helas! Quelle douleur a veoir le plus noble oncle qui
aujourd'ui vive, comme de trois roys, de six ducs et de tant
de contes, en assemblee mortele contre sa propre chair, et   25
les nepveux qui tant doivent de reverence a si noble oncle,
si comme a pere, contre lui en bataille! O noble sang de
France non reprouchié! Comment pourrois-tu, trés noble
nature, endurer--ja la journee ne puist venir--que tele
honte advieigne que ceulx qui estre seullent pilliers de   30
foy, sousteneurs de l'Eglise, par quel vertu, force et savoir
est toujours soustenue et pacifiee, et qui entre toutes
nacions sont nommez les trés chretiens acroisseurs de paix,
amis de concorde, vieignent ades a tel inconvenient?

    Or viens doncques, viens, noble duc de Berry, prince   35
de haulte excellence, et suy la loy divine qui commande
paix! Saisy la bride par grant force, et arreste ceste non

bragged about the noble blood of your princes, not your
tyrants, and reproached us for our manners worthy of Guelphs
and Ghibellines![4] Now they have sprung up on your soil.
The seeds are sown, they will not fail, your provinces have
already come to that. Lower your horns, because your glory   5
is gone!"

Ah, me! Sweet, suffering France! Are you really in
such peril? Indeed, yes! But there is a remedy. God is
merciful. All is not dead, although it is in danger of
dying.   10

Oh, Duke of Berry, Noble Prince, excellent father and
scion of royal children, son of a King of France, brother
and uncle, father of all the antiquity of the lily! How is
it possible that your tender heart can bear to see you, on
a given day, assembled in deadly battle array to bear pain-   15
ful arms against your nephews? I do not believe that the
memory of the great natural love of their fathers and
mothers, your much beloved deceased brothers and sisters,
will not naturally allow tears to flow like a fountain down
your face, and your noble heart not to break with pity so   20
much so that it will barely support you. Alas! What a
pity it is to see the noblest uncle alive, uncle of three
kings, six dukes and as many counts, in a mortal confronta-
tion against his own flesh, and the nephews who owe so much
reverence to such a noble uncle, like to a father, be in war   25
against him![5] Oh, noble and blameless blood of France! How
could you, your noble nature, allow--and may the day never
come--such a shame to occur, and that those who are the
pillars of faith, the supporters of the church, by whose
virtue, strength and wisdom it is always sustained and kept   30
in peace, and who are the most Christian among all nations,
developers of peace, friends of concord, to come to such an
unfortunate pass?

So, come, come, Noble Duke of Berry, Prince of High
Excellence, and follow the divine law which orders peace!   35
Take a strong hold of the bridle, and stop this dishonorable
army, at least until you have talked to the parties. So

[4]The feuds between the Guelphs (for the Church) and the
Ghibellines (for the Empire) were also mentioned in *Mutacion
de Fortune* (Solente, v.2, pp. 14-18). [5]The three kings are
Charles the Sixth of France, Louis of Anjou, king of Naples,
and Charles the Third of Navarre. The six dukes related to
Berry must be Burgundy, Brabant, Orléans, Visconti, Savoy,
and Austria. At least five of the following counts can be
called Berry's "nephews": Nevers, Armagnac, Alençon,
Clermont, Charolais.

honorable armée, au mains jusques a ce que aus parties ayes
parlé. Si t'en viens a Paris, en la cité ton pere ou tu
nasquis, qui a toy crie en lermes, soupirs et pleurs et te
demande et requiert. Vien tost reconforter la cité adolee,
et te avance avec la langue de correccion vers tes enfans   5
se tu les vois mesprendre, si comme bon pere, et les pacifie
en les reprenant, si que tu doiz et bien t'appartient, leur
enseignant raisons d'une partie et d'autre comment, quel que
soit leur descord, eulx, qui doivent estre pilliers, deffense
et sousteneurs de la noble couronne, et targes du royaume   10
qui onques ne leur meffist ne ne doit comparer ce que ilz
s'entredemandent, ne le vueillent destruire.

   Et pour Dieu! Pour Dieu! Noble duc, vueilles tost
advertir que--quoy que par divers langages soit a present
devisé en chacune partie, esperant de la victoire pour soy   15
de la bataille, en disant: "Nous vaincrons et ainsi
ouvrerons"--que trop est fole la vantise! Car ne doit estre
ignoree comme estrange, et non cogneue est la fortune de
toute bataille. Car quoy que de homme soit proposé, Fortune
y dispose. Et que valut jadis au roy de Thebes soy partir   20
vainqueur de la bataille, lui IIIe sans plus de chevaliers
et touz les siens mors laissiez ou champ, gisans avec la
multitude de ses ennemis desimé par glaives de ses parens et
princes? Dieux, quel victoire trop fu douleureuse! Le roy
d'Athenes navré a mort en bataille, que lui valu sa victoire?   25
Ne que prouffite en tel cas multitude de gens? Ne fu Xercés
desconfit, qui tant en avoit que vaulx et mons touz couvers
en estoient? Bon droit et juste querelle vault-elle donques?
S'ainsi estoit, le roy saint Loys, qui tant avoit eu de
belles victoires, n'eust pas devant Thunes esté desconfit par   30
les mescreans. Quel plus bel exemple est cognoistre que par
merveilleuse disposicion Dieu laisse encourir tout fait de
bataille, de la quelle le mal est certain, et le bien qui
avenir en puet gist en grant doubtance! Et ensurquetout,
quoy qu'en touz cas soit guerre et bataille trés perilleuse   35
et forte a eschever, n'est pas doubte qu'entre si prochains

come to Paris, to your father's city where you were born and
which cries to you with tears and sighs, asking and begging
for you to come.[6] Come quickly to comfort this suffering
city, and come to your children with correcting words if
you see them err, like a good father, and pacify them while   5
correcting them as you must appropriately do, teaching them
the reasons on one side and the other that, whatever their
disagreement may be, they, who should be the pillars,
defenders and supports of the noble crown, and the shields
of the kingdom which never harmed them, must weigh what they   10
ask from each other, must not destroy it.

    For God's sake! For God's sake! Noble Duke, please do
say soon that--although it is now discussed in various
tongues on each side that hopes for victory in the battle
and they all say: "We will win and work for it"--they are   15
bragging foolishly. For it must not be ignored that the
outcome of all battles is strange and unknown. For although
man proposed it, Fortune disposes it. For what good did it
do to the King of Thebes to leave as victor of the battle
with only three men and no more knights, with all his kin   20
dead on the field, lying with the multitude of his enemies
killed by the swords of his parents and princes?[7] God, this
victory was too painful! Was the victory of the King of
Athens, mortally wounded in battle, of any worth to him? Is
a multitude of men an advantage in such a case?[8] Was Xerxes   25
not defeated, although he had so many men that all vales
and hills were covered with them? Are a good reason and a
just quarrel of any value?[9] If it were so, the king Saint
Louis, who obtained so many beautiful victories, would not
have been defeated at Tunis by the infidels.[10] What better   30
example is it than to know that God, by marvellous disposition, lets all battles run their course, the outcome of
which is certainly evil, and whose resulting good is
extremely doubtful. And above all, although war and battles
are in all cases very dangerous and difficult to avoid, no   35
doubt that among such close kin, tied by nature in one bond

[6]John was born in Paris in 1340. [7]Adrastus, king of Ar-
gos--not of Thebes--was the only survivor of the famous war
of "The Seven against Thebes." [8]Codrus, last king of Athens,
sacrificed himself for his country. Also in *Fais et bonnes
meurs du sage roy Charles V* (Solente, v.1, pp. 186-87). [9]Xer-
xes, king of Persia, witnessed from Mount Aegaleos the defeat
of his fleet at Salamis (480 B.C.). According to Herodotus,
his armies amounted to more than two million men. Also in
Mutacion de Fortune (Solente, v.2, pp. 242-56). [10]Saint
Louis died of the plague at Tunis, the 25th of August, 1276.

parens, comme nature a conjoins si comme en un mesmes lien
d'amour, est trés perverse, non honorable et trés excommeniee
ne a bonne fin venir ne puet. Helas! Et s'il est ainsi,
ce que sy, que pour assez de causes et de querelles soient
souvent meues guerres et batailles, par plus fort et   5
meilleur raison en est trop plus par quoy doivent estre
fuyes et eschevees, et paix quise.

 Or vainque donques la vertu le vice! Si soit donques
voie trouvee de ramener a paix les amis par nature, ennemis
par accident. Helas! Qu'a Dieu pleust que la paine et   10
mise, que a present on desploie, feust ainsi employee a
querir paix comme elle est le contraire! Je croy que a
mains de coustz on y vendroit, et que de commun vouloir et
vraie union ceste armée feust convertie sur ceulx qui nous
sont naturels ennemis, si que celle part s'emploiassent les   15
bons feaulx François, non pas eulx entre-occire. Diex! Quel
joie seroit-ce! Et quelle trés haulte honneur a tousjours
au royaume!

 Ha, trés honnoré prince, noble duc de Berry, a ce
vueilliez entendre, car il n'est tant grant chose que cuer   20
humain vueille entreprendre par especial faicte en juste
entencion, a quoy il ne puist attaindre! Et se, tu, en ce te
travailles a toujours maiz, seras clamé pere du regne,
conserveur de la couronne et du trés noble liz, custode du
hault lignage, reserveur de l'occision des nobles, confort   25
du peuple, garde des nobles dames, des veufves et orphelins.
A la quelle chose le benoit Saint Esprit, acteur de toute
paix, te doint cuer et courage de tost le mettre a fin!
Amen. Et a moy, povre voix criant en ce royaume, desireuse
de paix et du bien de vous touz, vostre servante Christine,   30
meue en trés juste entente, doint veoir la journee! Amen.

 Escript le XXIIIe jour d'aoust, l'an de grace mil
CCCC et dix.

of love, they are perverse, dishonorable and to be condemned
if one cannot draw them to a good conclusion. Alas, and if
it has to be that wars and battles are begun for many reasons
and quarrels, then they should also be avoided and shunned by
better and more valid reasons, and peace should be sought. 5

So let virtue overcome vice now! Let one way be found
to bring to peace men who are loved ones by nature, and
enemies by accident. Alas! Would to God that the trouble
and the mobilization that is now displayed be used to seek
peace instead of the opposite! I believe the cost would 10
be less, and that this army, by a common will and true unity,
should be directed against those who are our natural enemies,
and that the good and faithful French should take care of
these people, and not kill one another.[1] God! What joy
this would be! And what high honor would it be to the 15
kingdom forever!

Ah, Very Revered Prince, Noble Duke of Berry, do hear
this, for there is nothing greater than what a human heart
wants to accomplish, especially in good intent, and cannot
manage to attain! And if you work constantly to that 20
purpose, you will be called the Father of this kingdom,
keeper of the crown and of the very noble lily, guardian of
the high lineage, protector of noble men against death, comfort of the people, guardian of the noble ladies, widows and
orphans. May the Blessed Holy Spirit, Author of all peace, 25
give you the heart and the courage to achieve such a thing!
Amen. And may He grant me, a poor voice crying in this
kingdom, wanting peace and welfare for all, your servant
Christine, moved by a very fair mind, the gift to see that
day! Amen. 30

Written the 23rd day of August, in the year of grace
1410.

[1]The dukes of Berry, Bourbon, and Orléans with the
count of Armagnac, made an alliance in Gien on April 15,
1410, and formed an army of 9,000 men. The purpose was to
attack John of Burgundy, rescue the king and the dauphin,
and restore them to power. John the Fearless, from July
onwards, was busy making his own military preparations.
The mobilization was brought to an end by a truce negotiated
by the duke of Berry in his castle of Bicêtre on November 10
of that year.

INDEX OF PROPER NAMES

Index of Proper Names